# Long Life and Prosperity Agenda

**Health, vitality, prosperity and fulfillment are God's will for us**

## GODDAY OJORE AGHEDO

**Long Life and Prosperity Agenda**

© **Godday Ojore Aghedo, 2016**

ISBN-10: 1544669569
ISBN-13: 987-1544669564

FIRST PUBLISHED: June, 2016

PUBLISHED BY:
Glomic Books Int'l
E-mail: globalimpactconsults@gmail.com
Tel: +2348054110176

# DEDICATION

I dedicate this book, first to MY LATE FATHER, BEN TEKA AGHEDO whose passion for the healing of the sick using his vast knowledge of the curative powers of nature, motivated me into the health profession. Dad, though you are gone to the world beyond, your legacies abound and they keep speaking aloud. It is enough consolation to know that, we are walking in the virtues you cultivated in us. The virtues of prudence, truth, honesty, hard work, discipline, self-control, patience, accountability, love & respect for mankind, determination, planning and strategy, proactive-ness, dedication & devotion, pragmatism, excellence mentality and the fear of God. You taught me wisdom, and through you I came to understand that, "The strongest people are not those who show strength in front of us; but those who win battles we know nothing about." Your passion was to bring healing and health to people, that is exactly what this book is aimed at.

Ultimately, I dedicate this book to the Holy Spirit, my Teacher, Helper, Inspirer, Comforter, and Leader; through whose involvements, I have always been empowered to put my thoughts and knowledge together in books, articles, and verbally.

# CONTENTS

# ACKNOWLEDGMENTS

In the first place, I regard in high esteem, my parents (Mrs Comfort Aghedo and Late Ben Teka Aghedo) for being the instruments by which I have been consistently shaped. They have both continued to be a great source of motivation to me. I appreciate my siblings whose love and sense of unity have remained unflinching and undaunted: Lucky, Catherine, Doris and Charity.

My unfathomable gratitude goes to Godfrey Omaoja (a friend and a brother indeed), Jane Igwe, Mrs Helen Aluede, Dr E. O. Nwoke, Dr Ehiremen Edobor, Mrs Hilda Hunter, Barr R. A. Orukpe, Mr S. E. Okojie, Mr Andy Adeke, Mr Mark Okondoh, Daddy David Ibadin (a man whose spirit of generosity has no match, in my opinion), Franklyn Imomoh, Ehis Okoufoh, Monday Oaikhena, Igbaragu Nelson, Lucky Eromosele Ebhodaghe, Joseph Omondiagbe and many other – whose names space would fail me to mention here.

# CHAPTER ONE
# GOD'S PLANS FOR MAN

God our creator and master planner of the universe operates outside time. He is not limited or restricted by time. He is the Alpha and Omega – the beginning and end. He declares the end from the very beginning; He is Omnipresent, Omnipresent and Omniscience. By the words of His mouth was everything created but He was not created. Through faith we understand that the worlds were framed, designed and fashioned by His infallible Word (Hebrews 11:1).

Like a wise architect, God must have a clear plan and picture of the kind of world to produce. After everything else had been created, He said, ***"...Let us make man in our image, after our likeness: and let them have dominion..."*** Genesis 1:26, KJV. That means that in virtually all respects, man is the image of God, man is like Him. This verse of the scripture reveals God's plans for man.

He wants man to be wise like Him
He wants man to live forever like Him
He wants man to exercise dominion over everything He has created
He wants man to be creative like Him
He wants man to live in abundance like Him
He wants man to fulfill dreams, goals and desire effortlessly like Him
He wants man to think like Him
He wants man to talk like Him
He wants man to relate like Him
He wants man to judge correctly like Him
He wants man to be visionary like Him

The list continues...

Now, part of God's plans is to have man live and prosper. Even after man fell from grace and abominations were committed by the offspring of Adam, God's plan for man to live was still very much intact. Cain murdered Abel and the Lord cursed him, but never allowed him to be killed.

*"And now art thou cursed from the earth,… And the LORD said unto him, therefore whosoever slayeth Cain, vengeance shall be taken on him sevenfold. And the LORD set a mark upon Cain, lest any finding him should kill him."*
**-Genesis 4:11-15, KJV**

In Job 1:12, God permitted Satan to wreak much havoc on Job, but never allowed him to touch his life; "And the LORD said unto Satan, Behold, all that he hath is in thy power; only upon himself put not forth thine hand…"

Again, we see in Numbers 21:8-9, "…the LORD said unto Moses, Make thee a fiery serpent, and set it upon a pole: and it shall come to pass, that every one that is bitten, when he looketh upon it, shall live…"

In the new testament, precisely in John 10:10, Jesus said that He had come to give man abundant life. This life, the God's kind of life – "zoe" begins here on earth, contrary to popular belief

Many folks including believers (in God) hold the opinion that long life is not a possibility on earth. They opine that eternal life begins after one's demise. Psalms 103:15-16 and 1 Peter 1:24 have been misinterpreted more often than not.
*"As for man, his days are as grass: as a flower of the field, so he flourisheth."*
**-Psalms 103:15, KJV**

*"For all flesh is as grass, and all the glory of man as the flower of grass. The grass withereth, and the flower thereof falleth away."*
**-1 Peter 1:24, KJV**

But Psalms 90:4 helps us understand the context better. It reads, **"For a thousand years in thy sight are but as yesterday when it is past, and as a watch in the night." KJV.** This means that a man may live a thousand years, but before the LORD it is just like a day. It also means that the number of years spent on earth, no matter how long (in the eyes of men) is nothing to compare with eternity with God.

Let's examine the position of Adam Clarke's Commentary, "Thou carriest them away as with a flood. Life is compared to a stream, ever gliding away; but sometimes it is as a mighty torrent, when by reason of plague, famine, or war, thousands are swept away daily. In particular cases it is a rapid stream, when the young are suddenly carried off by consumptions, fevers…; this is the flower that flourisheth in the morning, and in the evening is cut down and withered. The whole of life is like a sleep or as a dream. The eternal world is real; all here is either shadowy or representative. On the whole, life is represented as a stream; youth, as morning; decline of life, or old age, as evening; death, as sleep; and the resurrection as the return of the flowers in spring. All these images appear in these curious and striking verses, Ps 90:3-6."

However, my contention is that, God desires that we should live a considerably good number of years on earth, fulfilling His purpose before we are translated into the realm of eternity with Him. I believe that God's will for us is long life and prosperity on earth. God wants us to dominate, live, succeed, prosper and reign long enough to transform the earth, preparing it for the second coming of Jesus.

Prosperity is not a sin, it is not an anti-gospel, riches and wealth are not demonic, and it is a promise first to the believers. Its tendency of becoming a stumbling block to possessors if excessive attention is paid to it rather than God the giver; does not make it unworthy, unholy and undesirable. The problem is not with success, riches, wealth and prosperity, but the un-renewed heart of man. Apostle Paul, teaching the Corinthians how Jesus Christ had expressed concerns about their financial well beings, and had laid the foundation of riches and prosperity for them and by extension, the believers today, said:

*"For ye know the grace of our Lord Jesus Christ, that, though he was rich, yet for your sakes he became poor, that ye through his poverty might be rich."*

**-2 Corinthians 8:9, KJV**

The price for sin, sickness, disease and poverty has been paid in full. Christ was poor so that we can be rich. He died prematurely to redeem us and deliver long life to us. The earlier we accept this reality, the better for us and the church at large. Whether or not we dwell in this realm of bliss and glory does not alter the authenticity of the truth that Jesus Christ has fully paid the cost price for our liberty and fullness of life. The greatest problem of the end time church is IGNORANCE of what Jesus has accomplished in her favour.

We are no more to live in want, lack and insufficiency. All things are now ready. According to the level of our capacities, we are to obtain from the Lord all that we need. *"According as his divine power hath given unto us all things that pertain unto life and godliness, through the knowledge of him that hath called us to glory and virtue"* 2 Peter 1:3. Our greatest undoing is lack of relevant knowledge. ALL THINGS that are necessary for life and godliness have been made ready for every believer, but he or she can only have access through knowledge. Looking at verse four, you will understand that God wants us to be part of His divine nature. God's prosperity plan for man is not to be expected, it has been accomplished, key into it.

This is further established by Psalms 34:10, KJV, *"The young lions do lack, and suffer hunger: but they that seek the LORD shall not want any good thing."* Except you do not believe in the Word of God, it says that those who seek the LORD **shall** not lack **any** good thing. This is nothing else other than a promise and assurance of true prosperity. Psalms 84:11 (KJV) renders it thus, *"For the LORD God is a sun and shield: the LORD will give grace and glory: no good thing will he withhold from them that walk uprightly."* This passage makes it more specific, "...them that walk uprightly." And who are they that walk uprightly? The Christians of course! That settles the fact that prosperity is God's will and plan for every Christian.

# CHAPTER TWO
# KEYS TO LONG LIFE

God's original intent was to have been live forever like Him and with Him. This is because man was created for His pleasure in the first place. God is eternal in nature; therefore, created in His image after His likeness to be partakers of His divine nature, man was to live everlastingly. But sin (disobedience) brought in death, and abrogated man's access to God's presence. In fact he was casted out of the garden, cursed and subjected to labour and lifestyles that can't support or guarantee long life. However, God as time went by; set man's minimum earthly life-span at one hundred and twenty (120) years. This was called for and necessary too, since His Spirit cannot continue to strive with man (Genesis 6:3). This decree was as a result of the wickedness of the people during the time of Noah (Genesis 6:1-8). As man persisted in his evil, coupled with unending series of wars, this number continued to decline as observed by King David in Psalms 90:10.

But today, what is shocking is that for certain known and/or unknown reasons, people are rarely found living up to these years. Of course, you will agree with me that in our contemporary society, a man between the ages of 105-120 years has lived long. But I believe that it is possible for everybody to live long before the physical death.

As we count absolutely on God's grace, here are a number of principles that can enable as live long, on earth. Absolute adherence to these simple truths collectively, is the secret to long-life on earth. I call them the keys to long life. Let's examine them in briefly.

## KINDNESS AND HONESTY - PROVERBS 21:21

First and foremost, integrity is built on honesty and kindness. A dishonest man has no integrity. What is kindness? What is honesty? Kindness is to be greatly interested in the feelings and happiness of others. A kind person always seeks the good of others. He does not want to see people suffer-he rather prefers to share in it with them. On the other hand, honesty has to do with sincerity, truthfulness, not telling lies, being straight forward, stable and trustworthy. These characters in a man can produce life in him.

*"Be kind and honest and you will live a long life; others will respect you and treat you fairly."*

**-Proverbs 21:21, GNB**

Kindness and honesty, especially, form the foundation for everything that must last long. Apart from this, they earn you honour and kind treatment as well. Be sure that you are honest to your boss, parents, leaders, friends, co-workers, subordinates; the reward is long life. This extends to enjoying your wealth for a long time. Riches gotten by dishonesty lead you to death and then varnish (Proverbs 21:6).

**DON'T CURSE PARENTS - Proverbs 20:20**

Curse here represents insult or abuse. Parents here cover your biological, spiritual, political and traditional leaders as well as elders in general. Whoever curses his/her parent carries a curse of short life (or premature death) upon himself/herself-whether or not the parent speaks a word. This accounts for the sudden death of many young stars in our world today. Even after giving your life to Christ, having been a victim of cursing parents, there is a strong need to embark on restitution and reconciliation. They sure have a role to play in annulling that curse especially if they are still alive.

**"If you curse your parents, your life will end like a lamp that goes out in the dark."**

**Proverbs 20:20, GNB**

Just believing in God and coming to the church does not make you a child of God automatically. Even the devil believes and trembles. You have to be transformed. There is a Spirit of adoption, who must bear witness with our spirit that we are the children of God. There is a Power of 'son-ship,' given only by the Holy Spirit. Read John 1:14 and Romans 8:14 &16 for a better illumination regarding the above assertions.

Listen, many children and adults are guilty of this consciously or unconsciously. There are a number of ways one can curse (abuse) one's parent: (a) taking to them at the top of your voice. (b) Asking them questions for an answer to their questions if you are required to say YES or NO or needed to make a simple statement. (c) Murmuring and thinking evil of them-insulting them in your mind. (d) When you argue blindly or unnecessarily, as to make them liars-when they are actually correct. (e) Outright disobedience or giving them a poor quality of something you could have done better-deliberately because of anger. (f) Not paying attention to them when they speak to you (g) Looking straight into their eyes steadily, in anger as well as making jest of them by raising your eye-browns and such related facial gestures. (h) Walking out on them and despising them.

If you have fallen victim of any of the above points, the simple thing is to always meet them in love and humility to register your apology. In the case that you can't reach them any longer (due to death), you have to pray a serious prayer of mercy to God – to break the yoke of the curse-possibly go for deliverance, inviting other men of GOD. Nothing should be taken for granted. Do you know that it is disrespectful and insulting too, to delay the answering of the calls of parents or even sit back unnecessarily-when you are actually doing nothing important? It is my dear! At such occasions, you should apologize immediately.

**KEEP GOD'S LAWS - Proverbs 19:16**

Keep all the laws of God. Don't select. Breaking one is breaking all (James 2:10). The laws or commandments of God are met to guide and pattern our lives to suit the purpose of God. We must allow them perform their functions guiding us into LIFE-long life. Remember also that laws made by constituted authorities (religious bodies, government etc) are inclusive. They must though be man-made or constitutional laws which do not contradict that of God in any manner. Laws made by parents or communities, should be kept also.

**"Keep God's laws and you will live longer: if you ignore them, you will die."**

**Proverbs 19:16, GNB**

'Keep' here, means to be conscious of them or to live by them: and in it you can find life. It is deadly to ignore the laws of God either as a result of ignorance or fear of what it will cost to keep it faithfully. Learn now! Read the prayer of David in Psalms 119:36, "Give me the desire to obey your laws rather than to get rich" (GNB). This law should be kept not in the mouth or on the lips but in the heart-Psalms 119:11.

**OBEY THE LORD - Proverbs 19:23.**

When you get messages from the Lord, don't dare to fail in your obedience. Such messages can be through dreams, the scripture, other creatures, inward ministration or even a fellow believer. Whether convenient or not, you must obey God when you are sure that God is speaking. What it costs you doesn't matter-just obey the Lord. He is always right.

> **"Obey the lord and you will live a long life, content and safe from harm." Proverbs 19:23, GNB**

Please be cleared about the difference between "obey the Lord" and "Keep God's laws." The later also includes the laws or rules and regulations by authorities through God's guidance which are set to make the society orderly, outside Biblical or divine statutes. For example, laws made in the schools should not be broken etc. Read 1 peter 2:13-17 for further study. But the former, is more of a direct dealing with God than man-man situations, especially for ministers.

For instance, as a pastor or a Priest of God, when an armed robber or a blood-money maker brings you a lot of money as a gift and requesting your blessing; though unaware to you that he/she is ungodly; but if the Lord speaks to you not to take the money inwardly-how will you react? Rejecting the money is obedience to the Lord while accepting the money is gross disobedience to the Lord. I am sure that point is understood by you. Good! Let's proceed.

**MIND WHAT YOU SAY - PROVERBS 18:21[a]**

What you say is what you see; what you say is what you get. Life and death are in the power of the tongue. What you say has the capacity to offer you life or death. Be conscious of what you say. Be positive always in your speech. Don't say what you don't understand; otherwise you will experience what you don't understand. There is POWER in your words. Man has the power to create things (both abstract and concrete) by words just like God.

**"...I will do to you the very things I heard you say."**

**Numbers 14:28, NIV**

When you talk anyhow, you will end up anyhow. A woman had her son seriously sick, and continued to believe that her enemies have killed the child. In fears and lamentations, she had severally proclaimed her son dead falsely. These negative thoughts and confessions lingered on for days and eventually the boy died. The diagnosis was typhoid and blood inadequacy. There were several other folks of like ailment whose lives were spared by God through the same set of health workers, same drug administration and in the same hospital previously. But the question is: why have they failed this time? The answer to this likely question on your mind hit me when I learnt that, four days later, another child with the same defect was admitted but was discharged within 96-hours.

This is the truth: the woman in the former instance killed her son with her words of fear. Look, when you are sick always proclaim life upon yourself. Speak boldly that you won't die. Every morning when you wake up, make it your blood tonic to say: "I will not die, I will live long, and it is well with me." Always remember to borrow the words of King David, who said, "I will not die, instead I will live…" Psalms 118:17. In 2 Kings 4:26, the Shunamite whose son was dead said to Gehazi, "… everything is all right…" (NIV). The King James Version puts it thus, "… it is well…" That was what exactly happened. Her dead son came back to life, her confession was true – it became well with him. Read 2 Kings 4:35-36 for the complete story.

You sell LIFE more easily to DEATH by what you say. You procure exactly what you proclaim. What some people said had landed them in life imprisonment. What you say can either destroy or develop, exterminate or establish, break or make, tear down or build up, pull down or plant, condemn or construct, award death or award life. Don't joke with negative words, accept not negative prophecies and always remember that you are the best prophet of yourself – if you prophesy life, you will have life.

**"What you say can preserve life or destroy it…"**

**Proverbs 18:21, GNB**

Consider this rendition, *"the tongue has the power of life and death…"* Proverbs 18:21, NIV. Tongue here represents WORDS or what you say.

Hear Robert Schuller: "Sooner or later, those who win are those who think they can." In the same vein, sooner or later, those who LIVE LONG are those who SAY they can. Learn to think before you say a WORD especially when stressed out and distressed. If you want to live long, first speak the words in your mind and judge it immediately, then SAY it if it is capable of producing life. Listen to Abraham Lincoln, "When I am getting ready to reason with a man, I spend one – third of my time thinking about myself and what I am going to SAY..."

What you say in a hurry can make you worry. Say only what you mean and mean what you say. Don't worry when your health is tampered with; but always SAY what makes you worthy of good health (i.e. long life). Be positive in whatever you SAY, Read proverbs 16:24 on your own.

**RIGHTEOUSNESS – PROVERBS 11:30**

"Righteousness gives life, but violence takes it away" Proverbs 11:30.

Nothing else pays much more than righteousness on earth. There are more good promises to a righteous living that have been revealed. It pays to be righteous because it "pains" to live it. The righteous will definitely prosper on earth (Proverbs 11:28[b]). If you want to live long, don't pursue life, but righteousness. Long life is the first fruit of righteousness.

> **"Long life is the reward of righteousness; grey hair is a glorious crown." Proverbs 16:31**

Apart from producing life here on earth, righteousness can also award life in eternity with God, it doesn't disappoint. He that knows righteousness knows life but he that lives it out actually has it. Righteousness is a secret to long life and prosperity. It is an access key to a world of prosperity, divine health and vitality.

**WISE TEACHING – PROVERBS 13:14**

Pay attention to the teachings of the wise, they are good preservatives to life in times of danger. Time spent listening to wise teachings is not waste. Wise teachings prepare you to live long on earth, providing you with all it takes to cope with life challenges. Wisdom does not depend on your grey hair. So, listen to all that is wise, from the young or old, male or female.

*"The teachings of the wise are a fountain of life; they will help you escape when your life is in danger."*

**Proverbs 13:14**

Wise teachings open the eyes to an open door of long life. It also opens the eyes to see danger while still far away, as well as suggesting possible ways of overcoming it victoriously.

## SAY THE TRUTH – PROVERBS 12:19

Let's read this anchor passage together:

**"A lie has a short life, but truth lives on forever."**

Lies are shorter cuts to death, I mean premature death. Truth senses life and makes you live long. Truth brings justice (verse 17). Truth is a spiritual armor against powers and principalities that war against long life. Ephesians 6:14 recognizes it as a belt to hold fix all other armor for effective "warring." When you say the truth you scale through triumphantly over short life. Truth may be bitter but learn to say it – that shows how mature you are. The best kind of truth to tell is the bitter truth. Your flesh may not like it. Your body may become rebellious against you because of it, but never border. It is not a truth until it offends somebody, at least the devil. The best person to tell the truth is SELF. Tell yourself the truth. Do you have Christ, do you have Salvation? Say the truth always for it holds promises of long life. You will pay dearly for every truth you fail to say knowingly or unknowingly.

## GET WISDOM – PROVERBS 9:11

Wisdom is used in the scriptures about 233 times. It is from the Greek word "Sophia" which simply means the applications of knowledge. It's meaning also includes: cleverness, skillfulness and scientific knowledge. By a way of definition, wisdom is that which enables men to judge what are the best time and manner to secure the best ends. There are so many benefits attached to wisdom. But we are considering long life here.

Wisdom is of the lord, it comes from God, and everybody that asks for it can have it (James 1:5). It can give long life to its possessor.
"Wisdom will add years to your life" – Proverbs 9:11 (GNB). Solomon was reminded of the promises that accompany wisdom as taught by his father David in Proverbs 4:2-3; hence he chose to be blessed with wisdom as the principal thing (Proverbs 4:7); rather than asking for any other earthly acquisitions.

King David further taught that happy was the man who had wisdom and who had understanding (Proverbs 3:13). This reveals that wisdom ushers you into the realm of understanding. In reference to Proverbs 3:14-15, wisdom is more profitable than silver and gold; it has a higher value and net worth than jewels. You need wisdom, it makes life easy and things work out as well easily. There is abundant life in wisdom. Go tap it!

*"Wisdom offers you long life, as well as wealth and honor. Wisdom can make your life pleasant and lead you safely through it."*
**Proverbs 3:16-17, GNB**

Verse 18 of the above quotation, says that: the wise are happy because wisdom gives them life. You see, you cannot be truly happy unless you are truly living. But unfortunately, more people are simply existing rather than abundantly living the LIFE of Christ.

## QUALITIES OF DIVINE WISDOM

(1)   It is God given – James 1:5, 3:17; 1 Corinthians 12:8
(2)   It is based on reverence for God – Proverbs 9:10
(3)   It produces happiness – Proverbs 3:18
(4)   Produces obedience unto the Lord, it leads to holiness – Proverbs 3:7

## GENUINE REPENTANCE – EZEKIEL 33:14-16

Without apology we have too many unrepentant sinners in the modern church. The almost becoming constant incidence of premature deaths can be traceable to this ugly scenario. Listen to me; it is dangerous to come to the church without genuinely repenting, because the devil will be up against you. Genuine repentance brings long life. To be genuinely repented is to be born again.

No man can deceive God. There are three people you cannot deceive

(a) **GOD** – He is All-knowing, Omnipresent, Omnipotent and Omniscience.

(b) **SATAN** – he knows clearly those who are his and those who are totally God's. He knows those who still possess his properties. He knows those who are in the same club with him, he knows the true children of God, he knows those who confess Christ with their lips, but believe in Satan in their hearts. If you are his or not, he knows you can't deceive him.

(c) **YOURSELF** – nobody can actually deceive ONESELF; you can only be ignorant. You know within you whether you have been SAVED or not. You know within you whether you have genuinely repented (born again) or not. You may pretend, but you know the truth. Every man has an inward spirit which bears witness to anything he does or imagines or thinks about or says.

In the actual sense, you can't tell **GOD** a lie, you can't tell **SATAN** a lie and you can't tell **YOURSELF** a lie. Let's go a little further into the meaning of genuine repentance.

**WHAT IS GENUINE REPENTANCE?**

What does genuine repentance represent? How can it be identified? Who is genuinely repented?

First, it means to be fully or completely turned from IDOLS to GOD, serving the true God and waiting ready for the reappearing of Jesus Christ. The believers in Thessalonica are examples (1 Thess. 1:9-10).

Idols, I do not mean images alone. Self can be your idol; clothes can be your idol. Beauty and care of the body can be your idol. Money can be an idol to some other persons. I define an idol as anything you put before God or esteem higher than God. An idol is anything you exalt above the knowledge of God. It can be political power and positions, it can be education or ambitions, and it can be even your business or profit. Whether you agree with me or not, everybody has an idol he must get rid of. Genuine repentance is to turn away from them unto God alone. A complete "U – turn" must be made. Anything you love more than God is an idol; turn from it. In short, SELF is the first idol of a man, we must acquire the skills required to deal with the flesh.

Second, genuine repentance is to give back to the world (Satan) everything that belongs to it which you possess, and then, give completely to God, that which duly belongs to him alone: your life, your love and commitment, total submission of the body soul & spirit and true worship are examples. Zacchaeus has exemplified this in (Luke 19: 8 – 10). It also means to leave the old and present WAYS which lead to death and live in the NEW Way of CHRIST which leads to life.

Third, it means to constantly live in the consciousness of right doing (i.e. righteousness), including a burning desire to please the Lord in all things. It is to acknowledge your sins, asking for God's mercy and cleansing as soon as it is needed. King David is an example to emulate, Psalms 51:3-5. No pretense! Tell yourself the TRUTH and nothing but the truth.

There are many more scriptural examples you have to discover. Coming down to our immediate society, imagine a youth who has five opposite sex sexually immoral friends, but later decides to accommodate only one of them because he now goes to the church. Has such a youth truly repented? The answer is an emphatic NO. Such a youth has not genuinely repented. If a pagan who used to visit witch doctors for consultations becomes a believer in Christ; but still sends money through people to do the consultations for him/her – he or she has not genuinely repented. Genuine repentance changes your entire lifestyle – it makes you NEW and born again. You become a new creature with new features (2 Cor. 5:17).

Friends, this is the kind of repentance that produces life. A born again believer does not take anything for granted. He or she does not recognize "it doesn't matter".  And for your information brethren, it doesn't matter has become the matter arising. Whoever that has repented genuinely does not agree with the majority when they are wrong. He or she does not take part in wrong practices even when the world is adopting and making it an integral cultural possession.

For instance, he or she won't take part in exam malpractices even when pastors and reverends see it as a normal feature of an examination process. Even if proprietors who are pastors approve it, a genuinely repented believer will not take part in it. This could be detrimental to your admission at times anyway, including the other troubles but at last you will have life (breakthrough, and standing ovation by the world).

Genuine repentance does not agree to LOBBY for anything. It does not give or take bribes, it does not oppress, and it does not close its eyes in fear to injustice. It does not shut the mouth in fear to the evils of the society. It is at times very radical indeed. Don't cheat in any manner when you are truly repented (Ecclesiastes 7:7).

Dear friend, when all these are done, LIFE will germinate. That is the reward! Turn with me to the bible of Ezekiel 33:14-15;

*"... If he turns ... Or gives back what he stole...and follows the laws that give life he will not die but live."*

**Ezekiel 33:14-15**

Check yourself brothers and sisters! Ask yourself and answer yourself SINCERELY: "AM I GENUINELY REPENTED?" if your answer is YES, then you can be sure to have long life.

## LOVE GOD, OBEY GOD, BE FAITHFUL TO DO – DEUT. 30:20

Let me allow the bible to speak for itself;
*"Love the lord your God, obey him and be faithful to him, and then you and your descendant will live long in the land he promised to give your ancestors."*

**-Deut. 30:20, GNB**

I am sure it is very clear to you. Don't be an infidel – be faithful to God, don't betray God to the devil like many people are already doing.

# CHAPTER THREE
# THE WORD OF LIFE

In this chapter, we shall further x-ray the keys to long life, with special attention on the Word of God. John 1:1 makes it clear that Jesus is the Word and this is further entrenched by 1 John 5:7. Logically, if Jesus came to give life to mankind, invariable, the Word is for the same purpose. God will always send His Word, whenever there is need to intervene in the affairs of men. Man was in a sinful state, without hope and under the clutch of death. To bring man salvation and redemption, God sent His Word, which became flesh and dwelt among us (John 1:14; Matthew 1:21). Man was buffeted with sickness and diseases of all sort, and subject to destruction; but God sent forth His Word to heal and to deliver from the impending destructions (Psalms 107:20). God's Word has an invaluable potential for life.
.

**God's Word – JOHN 6:63**

Acceptance and adherence to the cautions of the WORD of God gives long life. Don't play down on the Word of God – the Bible. It is beyond mere write ups, it is a life-giving stream. The Word of God is life itself and a giver of life to the simple hearted, hear Simon Peter attesting to this fact:

> *"Lord, to whom would we go? You have the word that gives eternal life."* John 6:68, GNB

Total obedience to the Word of God will give you long life and eternal life. This is because the Word is truth and leads to righteousness. It does mislead not! The WORD is a source of the spirit that gives life, and life itself is spiritual.

> *"This spirit gives life….the words I have spoken to you are spirit and they are life."*
> **John 6:63, NIV**

Don't doubt the Word of God for they hold the solutions to your difficulties, whether read or spoken, the Word of God is ever active and life-giving. Many people carry the Bible but only a few acknowledge the power of life in the Word. Many people die prematurely because they have died spiritually of the starvation of the Word of God; for the spirit controls the physical.

Your life prospers in most cases in direct proportion to the level of the prosperity of your soul (3 John 2). The Word of God is the most nutritious and nourishing food to the Spirit and Soul.

The Word of God in you and you abiding by the Word is like an open cheque into the treasures of God. You will have life if you write it on the check. "Anything" you ask for is granted. When you abide by the Word of God, you receive the power to ask for anything (long-life, wealth, healing, name it) and you will receive them.

*"If you remain in me and my word remains in you, then you will ask of anything you wish and you shall have it."*

-John 15:7,
GNB

It is true but as sure as that is, it is worthy of note that "IF" and "THEN" were logically and sensitively used. This usage infers conditionality. This accounts for why many believers do not enjoy the blessings that come with the WORD. You have to do one thing in order to get the other. Abide in the Lord first, let the Word abide in you and then, you can talk of partaking in the blessings thereof. Do accept the Word of God wholly. The amount of life in you is directly proportional to the amount of the Word of God in you. Spiritually speaking every time you hear and accept the Word of God you gain more life.

## HOW TO TAP LIFE FROM THE WORD OF GOD

There is abundance of life which we have to tap each time we hear the Word of God.

## BELIEVE!

This is the only HOW... You must believe the Word of God, Jesus Christ having told His Disciples that His words gave life, said further: "Yet there are some of you who don't believe" (John 6:64). Believe the Word of God, whether it appears difficult or not, whether it appears possible or not – just believe, trust and obey. There is an unspeakable power of life in BELIEVING the Word of God. It takes conviction to believe; and believe, conversion; and conversion, the reward of long life.

On the other hand, permit me to open your eyes to the fact that this same WORD is Jesus Christ.

*"In the beginning was the Word, the Word was with God, the Word was God. He was with God in the beginning. "*

-John 1:1-2

Do you notice the stress on the "W" in the "word"? Do you also notice the personification of the "WORD" by the use of the pronoun "HE" in verse two? Read verse three now! This is therefore enough proof that Jesus is the Word. Everything in the Bible points to Jesus Christ. Before Christ my Lord became Man, He was the Word. If the Word was God and Jesus was God; then Jesus is the Word. Do you understand?

To elucidate this further, words are meant to instruct, teach, and show "ways". Some ways lead to life others to death. Some words show up ways that lead to life, thus the scriptures in John 14:6 "...I am the way the truth and the life..." proves that Jesus, the way to life, is the Word. The Word of God can give you life because that is the mission of Jesus Christ. Turn with me to the gospel of John chapter ten verse ten.

*"I have come in other that you may have life – life in all its fullness."*

Take the Word of God seriously. Jesus is the Word, the Word is not preached for nothing, it is meant to strengthen you. It is meant to revive you, to restore and install life in you, to resurrect you, to renew, to revamp and rejuvenate you, to empower and to make you strong and healthy. It is also meant to heal you (Exodus 15:26).

Jesus is the Bread that gives life (John 6:25, 48). This food (the bread) does not spoil, it does last long and it gives eternal life (John 6:27). This food (the bread) is the Flesh and Blood of Jesus Christ (John 6:50 – 58). Like the disciple describe the eating of this food as a hard teaching (John 6:52, 60), many believers in our days have also tagged the Word of God as difficult to believe and follow (Obey). This is the reason behind the limited miracle and healing in our days.

Records of death here and there! Let's go back to the Word, let's see Jesus Christ from Peter's point of view and declare like him that Jesus Christ has the Word of LIFE (John 6:68).

Listen to me, this food cannot be egested it remains and continually produces life if you can eat it (accept it, believe it). Rice, beans, yam, melon and "ema" will digest and be egested. But the Word of God will digest when ingested and remain. If it does not remain life will be terminated. In the time past God gave manna, our ancestors ate, yet they died. But the present day manna (the food that comes from heaven) is Jesus Christ (the Bread). Those that will eat will not die but will live long (John 6:23, 58). Your attitude concerning the Word of God must change, if you must have life that lasts.

Going back to how we can tap this life you need to believe Jesus Christ, the Word. This is the desire of God Who sent Him (John 6:29), to believe Christ - and the reward is long life (John 6:40). In verse forty seven, Jesus declares: "I am telling you the truth: he who believes has eternal life."

BELIEVE is the crux of the matter. Believe in God, believe in Jesus Christ, believe in His word and you will live long. Don't select, accept all. When this is done, Jesus will give life to your mortal body. He will restore all your virtues that are stolen or lost. He will restore them! When you are at the verge of death in the spiritual, He will revive you and re-fan you to flame: by the Word. When things are falling apart and your heart broken He will join them together through the Word. Jesus is the source of life!

# CHAPTER FOUR
# DYING TO LIVE

The last secret of long life I want to disclose in this book is suffering, enduring and dying with Christ daily. Let us read our text quickly, from 2 Timothy 2:11.

*"This is a faithful saying: for if we died with him we shall also live with him."*

To die with Christ is to identify with Him in all aspects. To die with Christ is to mortify the flesh and hearken not to its desires. It means to be dead to sin and the pleasures of this world.

Beloved, the true situation seems like we have two natures, but the two natures do not rule the body at the same time. These natures, did Jesus put upon Himself to show the relationship between them. In Galatians 5:16; the Spirit and the human natures are identified, these are always in serious contention (verse 17). The human nature has its culture and practices, which lead to the death of the spirit (verse 12-21). Remember we mentioned in chapter three that the Spirit produces life (John 6:63). That is why Saint Paul told the Romans in chapter eight verse six that to be controlled by the human nature brought death while to be controlled by the Spirit brought life.

On the cross of Calvary, Jesus carried our sins and died with them, these, defiled Him which made God (whose eyes can't behold sin) forsake Him for the moment (Mark 15:34). When He was resurrected after burial, He rose with a brand new life and body which is immortal. Whoever share in His death qualifies to share in His glory and life (Romans 8:17).

Hence, when the human nature is alive, the spirit is dead (the person has no life). When the spirit is alive, then the human nature is dead – the dying with Christ – this is the true life. If there is no death, there can't be 'a same spirit' which brought Him back to life raising you to life likewise (Romans 8:11).

Now the day you are baptized or choose to be a Christian, you are initiated into a union with Christ's death (Romans 6:30). The immersion process during baptism therefore signifies being buried and sharing His death; so that, like He was raised, at your rising from the river of baptism, you receive God's glorious power and ability to live a new life (verse 4). This new life is freedom from the power of sin. You now have a new nature of holiness, and sin no longer controls you. Your flesh, the human nature no longer is your master, you no longer live under the law (of sin) but under the grace of God. At this point, you receive the visa or letter of transfer from death to life, you are no longer moved or excited by iniquity – nothing good or pleasurable is seen of it, you now hate sin and will not look to its side (Romans 6:6-14). This is the true death to sin with Christ, when your tastes, passions and interests change for better.

*"for since we have become one with him in dying as he did in the same way we shall be one with him by being raised to life as he was" – Romans 6:5.*

Here is another definition of dying with Christ: when you were in the world, just as you surrendered yourself (deliberately or not) as a slave to sin (or impurity) and wickedness for devilish purposes; now as a Christian, surrender yourself entirely as a slave to holiness for godly purposes (Romans 6:19). The wages of sin is death but there is life eternal, in union with Christ (Romans 6:23).

Dying with Christ demands total repentance and newness of heart, character and your entire being (2 Corinthians 5:17). You must put to death the desires of the flesh, the old man that work in you, such as sexual immorality, indecency, lust, evil passions, greed, anger, hateful feelings, obscene talk etcetera (Colossians 3:5-10). The death of the aforementioned practices leads to long life.

A seed must first die before germinating. I accompanied my father to his yam farm sometimes ago, to harvest the yams. While I was digging a particular tuber of yam: I discovered a putrefied and dried piece of yam surrounding it. After critical observation, I discovered that, the tuber of yam I was harvesting emanated from this useless and lifeless one, being the original seed planted. Immediately I recalled this scripture:

*"...a grain of wheat remains... a single grain unless it... dies. If it does die, then it produces many grains"*

**John 12:24**

There is life in dying first. There is life in death, just as a seed that doesn't die can't germinate or reproduce, no man can germinate or reproduce new life without crucifying the old-life. Power must change hands and character must change too

.

**REASONS FOR CHRIST'S DEATH**

Jesus Christ did die because He chose to. He was sent to die – to die for a people and for a purpose, His death was a missionary journey, not just to prove that He could resurrect. It goes beyond giving God our Father glory and manifesting His power. Let's examine three reasons for Christ's death in the following subtopics.

1. **To Destroy the Power of Death – Hebrew 2:14**

According to verse nine, He humbled Himself and accepted to suffer and taste death for everyone. Therefore, in verse fourteen;

*"Since the children have flesh and blood, he too shared in their humanity so that by his death he might destroy him who holds the power of death – that is, the devil."*

2. **To Reconcile Sinners To God – Romans 5:10-11**

Christ's death restored our friendship with God. While we were enemies, God loved us and manifested it by sending His Son. This is the hope of life which we have. Turn with me to the bible passage:

*"For if, when we were Gods enemies, we were reconciled to him through the death of his son, how much more, having been reconciled, shall we be saved through his life!" – verse 10 (NIV)*

Reconciliation is a journey through death to life, reconciliation is a mark of victory, and it is a bold step to climb higher in every endeavour of one's life. God has set an example of it. Please before you read the next chapter, go and reconcile with anybody that **HAS OFFENDED YOU** and that you have offended, including God. We have always offended God. We sinned against Him! Yet as big, mighty and magnificent as He is, He took (or initiated) the step of reconciliation; even while our actions made us His enemies, He yet called Himself our friend. If God (the Father) could do that, you have no excuse, no reason, whatsoever, not to forgive and reconcile with all those that offended you or that you offended.

You will find this book more interesting, if only, you can hear God telling you to reconcile now. It brings peace and joy to your soul and to your family. Reconciliation links you up to life and God's blessing. God took an extra-mile by sending us a Gift – Jesus Christ. You too do the same; send a precious gift to that person with whom you live maliciously. Gift work like magic! Don't neglect it, take a step! This is an opportunity to get promotion from God. Just pause a while and think – reason with me: RECONCILIATION IS NOT COMPLETE UNTIL IT IS RECYCLED TO FORGIVENESS AND EVENTUAL UNCONDITIONAL LOVE. Reconciliation always culminates in intimate friendship and communion.

3.    **To Gain For Sinners, the Resurrection of the Body – 1 Cor. 15**

Having been reconciled, we are brought into relationship with God. We have been united with God again through Christ's death. Because of this union, we shall be resurrected with Christ to life. People die today because they share in the sin (disobedience) of Adam, likewise, we shall be raised to life (or made righteous) if we share in Christ's death and the power of his resurrection.

**ONE MORE LESSON**

Well and good, we have learnt a good number of secrets to long life, but just before we continue to the next chapter, let's learn a lesson from a professor of philosophy. He teaches us how short the life on earth is and how contradictory it is; following the fact that life on earth consists of mysterious injustice and frustrations; out of this frustrations, he taught, "life is useless" (Ecclesiastes 1:2). I guess he built this point on what Ecclesiastes 5:15 insinuates;

*"We leave this world just as we entered it – with nothing. In spite of all our work there is nothing we can take with us."*

Despite the pessimism of the philosopher about life, he encourages everybody to work hard (Ecclesiastes 11:4, 6). Welcome to the lesson from Professor Solomon David-Jesse, a king and philosopher, from the UNIVERSITY OF LIFE; he said,

*"Be grateful for every year you live. No matter how long you live, remember that you will be dead much longer. There is nothing at all to look forward to. Our bodies will return to the dust of the earth and the breath of life will go back to God, who gave it to us."*
**Ecclesiastes 11:8; 12:7, GNB**

Let me tell you the truth, whether you live long here on earth or not, matters but it is not the ultimate; eternal life is the most important, Eccl. 2:5-6. We pray for long life on earth; but it is better to live shortly on earth and live long (eternally) in heaven than to live long on earth and loss eternal life in heaven. Nevertheless, it is much better to live long on earth as well as to make everlasting life. In fact, this is God's design and desire for us.

Therefore, what you do with your life on earth, whether short or long, will count on the last day. Be conscious of the life after this one on earth, it is sweeter. It is like the delayed wine at the wedding in Cana (John 2:10). It is better to die (mortify the flesh, self-denial of worldly pleasures, deliberate refrain from sin and all ungodliness) now and live then at Christ's glorious re-appearance. Think about your life now and make amend where necessary! Christ will come again to judge all mankind (Eccl. 12:14).

There is a way this life can be lived now, to profit you later. It is still part of the lesson from professor S. of UNILIFE (University of Life). In Ecclesiastes 12:13, he gives a profound insight into the main essence of man's existence on earth.

*"....here is the conclusion of the matter, Fear God and keep His commandments, for this is the whole duty of man."*
**Ecclesiastes 12:13, NIV**

To buttress his point on the whole duty of man, which is to live our lives in total reverence and obedience to God, a life that brings Him glory; here is a poem by me, titled "The duty of Man."

## THE DUTY OF MAN

The world is beautiful,
not everybody is dutiful.
The world is perfect,
but not every work is perfect.

Though beautiful and perfect,
we have a duty to perfect.
Though everything is alright,
we have so much to do at night.

He has done everything,
yet of us He requires, something.
If He has completed it for us,
what exactly does He require of us?

He did nothing, but for something.
He proposed a purpose for everything.
Purpose fulfilled of all creatures but man.
He has been disappointed by man.

What exactly does he require of man?
Dominion is in the power of man,
Man is to live a godly life,
man is to praise God all his life.

# CHAPTER FIVE
## SIX 'S' OF GOD'S BLESSINGS

Long life is God's blessing to man. Prosperity is a blessing from God. In fact, every good and perfect gift comes from the LORD (James 1:17). This chapter highlights briefly six standards which must be met to obtain God's blessings, which could be long life, prosperity, promotion, spiritual growth, financial open doors, marital breakthroughs, and material supply etc. Outside God's grace, life is all about principles, immovable standards. Whoever meets them, whether a believer or not, gets blessed.

This is what I mean: if Mr. A, a righteous Christian leader refuses to work even when he has the opportunity, but believes GREATLY that God will bless him all the same, his lack of work has countered or defied his faith. However, if Mr. B goes to work coupled with his faith, no matter how little, he is likely to be honoured and blessed by God first. Forget the measure of their beliefs, even the devil believes greatly in God and trembles too; but faith without work is vain and dead (James 2:19-20).

God does not encourage laziness. He that doesn't work should not eat; God Himself has set an example during the creation. He worked having spoken the words. It came to pass that there was light as He commanded; other creatures showed up in like fashion. However, when He commanded that there should be all kinds of vegetation on earth, the Bible says that it was done. God saw it and was pleased Genesis 1:11-12.

Please understand this truth, in Genesis 2:5 it is recorded that there were no plants on earth and no seeds had sprouted. This was because of two reasons (a) No rain (Vs. 5b) (b) nobody to cultivate the land (vs. 5). In other words, there was need for God to WORK further, in order to satisfy His need. God worked, now in verse seven, He came down, took some soil and made man out of it, and He didn't stop there. He in verse eight then planted a garden; He cultivated a garden: from where He made a beautiful tree to grow (Vs. 9). Friend, you can understand now that God worked to make the creatures manifest physically. Thus man is a fashion of God's empyreal Hands. What a privilege! Read Genesis 2:19, 21:22.

Are you still with me? Okay! Let's take one more proof that God worked, from Genesis 2:1-2. He finished His work and rested. "God ended His work..." it is true that when you speak, God answers and things happen (Spiritually in most cases) but you need to work to make it materialize. WORK IS THE TOOL FOR TRANSFORMING SPIRITUAL BLESSINGS INTO MANIFESTING IN THE PHYSICAL REALM. It is the conversion of God's answer to a tangible blessing or visible blessing.

Don't deceive yourself! Man must work, directly or indirectly in order to experience the tangible blessings of God. That is the importance of the principles we want to discuss now, He that works is qualified to eat. Man has been under a command to work hard as to survive. Hard work is not a curse, but laziness attracts a curse. Your REWARD is directly proportional to your WORK (1 Corinthians 3:8). God blesses us lavishly, but the proof of our readiness to receive the blessings is WORK - the actual evidence of our faith.

## OBEDIENCE + WORK = SUCCESS

Like chemical equations (in Chemistry), this is a spiritual equation which satisfies spiritual principle of breakthrough and growth, when your obedience is complete and you react it with WORK, a spiritual reaction is ignited which produces success in the physical realm; good success at that.

Therefore brethren, if God with all His power and majesty does not depend only on the power of His Word to do everything without labour and work, what about you? As a matter of fact, God chose to work to teach us its significance. However, work was the prescribed solution to the curse upon the earth, which can bring man to poverty and wretchedness (Genesis 3:19). Idleness has always been a curse and will always be, it is wrong to support men who will neither work nor assume their own responsibilities.

*"...if any would not work, neither should he eat."*
**-2 Thessalonians 3:10, KJV**

Nevertheless, be careful not to be busy bodies (2 Thess. 3:11). The Greek word, "Periergazoma" means to be busy about useless matters.

This is where obedience to God becomes a key player. Listen to God's instructions and work by the following principle, with His Word providing the needed guidance. Here is what Bill Vaughan has to say, "Retirement, we understand, is great if you are busy, rich and healthy; but then, under those conditions, **WORK** is great too".

I agree absolutely with Abraham Lincoln on his point, "You have to do your own growing no matter how tall your grandfather's was." This goes to the children of successful people. Don't depend on the wealth of your parents, cultivate your own field. A true child of a successful father does not only think of inheriting his father's wealth, he thinks more of becoming like his father and possibly greater by his personal WORK(s). Everybody has got the stamina and ability to acquire his or her desire. "The greatest good you can do for another is not just share your riches, but reveal to them their own" (Benjamin Disraeli).

### So, what are the six 'S's of God's blessings?

1. Seek for it
2. Stay upon God for it
3. Serve for it
4. Strive for it
5. Soft pedal for it
6. Sow for it

# CHAPTER SIX
## SEEK FOR IT

To seek is to ask for, to search for, to look for, and to go after something. You need to seek for the blessings of God. If you don't seek, you can't find. Matthew 7:22 says that everyone who asks will receive and anyone who seeks will find. Little wonder, many people don't receive the blessings of God simply because they do not ask, and have not found the blessings simply because they have not sought for it. The idea of seeking and finding connotes desire. A man who does not desire long life may not have it. In the same vein, a man who does not desire prosperity may not have it. It is natural to misuse or give negligibly little or no value to what one does not desire. Therefore, to be prosperous, you must desire it.

God knows what is good for us, that we need, but we have the duty to ask or seek it.

**"...How much more then, will your Father in heaven give good things to those who ask him!"**

**Matthew 7:11[b]**

The problem with believers today is that they seek through the wrong way; as a result, they don't receive their heart desires. There is a biblical method of seeking prosperity, which everybody must adopt in order to obtain results. Some people want to kill themselves because of money, fame, power, positions, and life. Depending on their abilities and hard work, some depend on what they call "godfather." I don't need an earthly "godfather" to get divine promotion. If you are seeking for promotion or protection or power or position and you are relying on a man, you will be utterly disappointed. Looking unto man for God's blessings is the reason you have not found it. We do not prevail by the arms of flesh. "It is better to trust in God than to put confidence in man" Psalms 118:8. It is God who gives power to get wealth, there are no two ways about it (Deut. 8:18).

At times people get what they want through "god-fatherism" and yet cannot find the peace in such acquisitions. When you seek God's prosperity through the wrong way, what you get is the actual container of the blessing without the content (peace). When you seek and get a child through the wrong channel, the child can't bring you joy but sorrows. What therefore is the essence? You don't need to offer a bribe to get promoted at your work place. In fact, the real thing you NEED does not have the potential to pass through a wrong road and survive. "I can't pay money to get what I am qualified to have in Christ Jesus" that is the confession of a true seeker of God's own blessings. You don't seek prosperity looking unto man. Prosperity does not come by mere hard work alone. Prosperity is not a product of luck, it comes from God.

**THE UNFAILING WAY TO SEEK...**

Now, how do we correctly seek prosperity or God's blessings in general? What is the guaranteed way to securing all that we seek of the Lord or ever desire? Well, the answer is simple: **seek the Giver, not the gift.** Seek the giver of prosperity, don't seek prosperity itself. Only what is given to man by God belongs to him. It is vain to seek earthly treasures and goods without recourse to God, the Source and Giver of all good things.

*"But seek ye first the kingdom of God, and his righteousness: and all these things shall be added unto you."*
**Matthew 6:33, KJV**

This is the unfailing general formula for finding God's blessings quickly. Do you want to marry? Are you looking for admission into tertiary institution? Is it office promotion or good health (healing)? What do you need, fruit of the womb, financial breakthrough, deliverance, personal house, wisdom and honour or long life? Forget all that and just seek God and righteousness. You will have the packages delivered to you. **God's long life and prosperity agenda are delivered effortlessly by seeking God and His righteousness.**

Man may grant you promotion, but he can't guarantee sustenance and survival of your life. Men may bestow lots of goods on you, but they can't guarantee your peace and fulfillment. Do you understand my point? Good! No wonder John 6:63 states that man's power is of no use at all. It consumes too much spiritual, physical and mental energy to seek these needs one after the other. But amazingly, seeking first (a) God's kingdom and (b) God' righteousness, entitles you to meeting ALL your needs (long life, prosperity, power, fame, abundance, peace, joy etc.). Does it sound unbelievable? Please believe it, that is how it works.

God's business must become our business; His passion, our passion, and His delight, our delight. We must be radically engaged in His soul winning agenda, to fully enjoy His long life and prosperity agenda. The advancement of His kingdom in all ramifications should become our utmost desire, to see His prosperity agenda unfold to us.

**The Place of Prayer...**

Prayer is very inevitable in seeking the Lord. The more time we spend in the place of prayer to God, the more glorious our lives become. The place of prayer is the place of answer to all that we seek in life. Prayer is our way of expressing our TRUST in only God. Concerning all of our needs, our first and last steps should be taken in prayers to God Almighty.

1 Samuel 1:9-18 presents us with a practical example. Here we see Hannah seeking God's intervention by prayer, "Hannah continued to pray to the Lord for a long time... she was praying silently: her lips were moving..." (Vs 12, GNB). She remained faithful to God in spite of the troubles she passed through for being childless. However, she sought to get a child but through God first in her life. Of course, she got the child. No one who sincerely turns to God in faith gets turned down.

*"I asked him for this child, and he gave me what I asked for."*
**1 Samuel 1:27**

In consonance with the promise in Matthew 6:33, God gave her five other children.

*"The Lord did bless Hannah, and she had three more sons and two daughters..."*
**1 Samuel 2:21**

By seeking God's kingdom and His righteousness, you are seeking the master key to all doors of His prosperity and blessings.

Let's examine the choice of King Solomon in 2 Chronicles 1:7-10. God gave him the opportunity to request anything. He (Solomon) knew that if he sought wealth, he would also need to seek long life and protection later on in life. God is Wisdom and only He can give it. James admonished that if you want to get wisdom, you seek God (James 1:5). It therefore implies that Solomon sought God in wisdom and for this wise choice, God blessed him with what he needed including the ones he didn't request, such as prosperity, protection, popularity and longevity.

*"...I will give you wisdom and knowledge and in addition: I will give you more wealth, treasures and fame than any king has ever had before you or will ever have again."*
**2 Chronicles 1:11-12, GNB**

Take note of **AND IN ADDITION** in the above passage. When you seek God first you get ADDITIONS in your heavenly package. We are discussing the reward or importance of seeking Christ before and above His blessings. Jesus Christ is an embodiment of grace and treasures. In Him there is joy, long life, prosperity, success, breakthroughs of all magnitude and all that man needs for a triumphant life on earth. When you have Jesus you are protected. When you have Jesus, you are healed. When you have Jesus, your needs are met - God supplies all your needs, through Christ, according to His abundant wealth (Philippians 4:19).

Seek Jesus first! There was a twenty – six year old girl who got infected by HIV/AIDS through rape exercise. Having tested positive, she refuse to believe the medical report. She was a committed Christian and was raped on her way to the church, one night; this girl went home and did not bother about taking good care of herself. She didn't pray for financial favour to enable her meet some needs. She was not discouraged and did not stop going to church to serve God.

Surprisingly, this girl served God much more, this time; she continued to seek God, abandoning her pains and desires. Guess what? After sometimes, she went back for the test, and she tested negative. There was confusion in the hospital. So she went to another hospital and still tested negative. Miracle! It is real! She didn't ask for healing from the HIV/AIDS infection, she sought God, she found Him, and He healed her, that's how it works! Ask and you shall receive; seek and you shall find; knock and the door shall be opened unto you (Matt. 7:7).

# CHAPTER SEVEN
## STAY UPON THE LORD

Staying upon the Lord, speaks of ABSOLUTE TRUST in God. It talks of unwavering faith in the person and capabilities of God. To stay upon God is to take Him for His Word and dwell in the comfort of His promises. We must learn to stay upon the Lord for whatever our needs may be, through: reverence for Him, obedience to His Word, supreme trust in His name and confidence in His power to fulfill His promises. It takes ONLY God to bring His Word to fulfillment in our lives.

*"Who is among you that feareth the LORD, that obeyeth the voice of his servant, that walketh in darkness, and hath no light? Let him trust in the name of the LORD, and stay upon his God."*

**Isaiah 50:10, KJV**

The "darkness" in the above passage signifies: problems, tough times, trials, persecutions, failures, delays, setbacks, pains and sicknesses, to mention but a few. Your own could be mountainous obstruction or obstacles. It could be disappointments or late marriage. Honestly, these things are stepping stones to uncommon and unusual success. Every Christian passes through dark paths at one point or the other, But I have a message for you: if you trust and stay (rely) upon God, your light will come sooner than your expectation. Whatever path of darkness God allows you to tour, is surely for your ultimate good (Romans 8:28). You only need to stay upon Him.

Therefore, to obtain God's blessings and secure a place in His long life and prosperity agenda, you have got to trust in Him and stay upon Him. Please WAIT ON, to take delivering of your portion in the prosperity of the end-time church.

*"But those who trust in the Lord for help will find their strength renewed. They will rise on wings like eagles; they will run and not get weary; they will walk and not grow weak."*

**Isaiah 40:31, GNB**

The origin Hebrew word for "Renew" is "Chalaph" which means: spring up, grow up, sprout, go forward, change or strike through. I want you to replace RENEW with each of these words, re-read it and imagine the magnitude of the effects or turn around God intends to make in the life and statuses of those that will trust and stay upon Him.

From Isaiah 50:10, we can outline two fundamental requirements under the stay-upon-the-Lord-rule for plugging into God's prosperity plans, followed by one sure effect. They are:

1. Fear or honour God
2. Obey the Words of His servant. After these, you can now
3. Stay upon God, trust Him and rely on Him for your supplies
4. Light will shine on your path. This is God's answer. Light is the answer and cure for darkness. Prosperity is not a function of luck but light. Light signifies insight, knowledge, understanding, direction, progress, speed in advancement and breakthrough.

In conclusion, to stay upon God also means to be patient. You need to be patient after you have done the will of God; to receive the fulfillment of His promises (Hebrew 10:36). In other words, don't give up on doing well. Every good deed you do equals 10-steps towards your reward. Don't give up or be weary in doing well to people, for in due season, you shall have your inevitable rewards (Galatians 6:9). Don't give up on good deeds!

Let's close with: "Many of life's failures are people who did not realize how close they were to success when they gave up" (Thomas Edison). My dear, the more good you do, the closer you become to your breakthrough. Thomas Edison also said, "Our greatest weakness lies in giving up; the most certain way to succeed is always to try just one more time." Please do good just one more time each time "giving up" becomes the only alternative. Don't give up when you can get up. Don't give up if you can get up. But I believe that you can get up if only you will.

# CHAPTER EIGHT
## SERVE FOR IT

God places great priority on service both to Him and to one another. Service is the gateway to exaltation. It is the first rung on the ladder to the throne. There is reward in serving the Lord. There is fulfillment in rendering one form of service or the other. God demands our worship in Spirit and truth (John 4:24), and service can be a spiritual act of worship. Service is also doing exactly what God sent you to do. In doing what God has sent you to do, you are nourished and replenished constantly. That is what Jesus Christ meant when He said:

*"...My food is to do the will of Him who sent me and to accomplish His work."*

**John 4:34, RSV**

How can you say that you love God who is unseen when you hate your brothers (1 John 4:20)? In the same way, how can you say that you serve God when you don't serve your one another or even our leaders? Leaders such as we find in the churches, schools, political and traditional terrains.

To serve does not necessarily make you a servant or slave. Here, I am concerned with the delivering of service to God and humanity. We must also learn to serve God through people..., serve your leaders, pastors, parents and heads at various cadres. If you have not served, you can't be a successful leader. A good follower is a good leader. The period of serving or following (i.e. followership) is God's own time for working out your promotion. You can't see God to serve Him; but the glory goes to Him for every good you do to the least of your fellow human being (Matt. 10:42; Mark 9:41). There are some things that are only obtainable on the altar of service, thus, it is a very vital part of Christian worship unto the Lord.

Therefore, serve your master as if he were God. If you are a labourer, do your work as if you are doing it for God. If you are a teacher, teach thoroughly as if you are teaching God. If you are a cook, prepare the meal as if Christ were the guest. If you are a sales representative, be transparent; give a sincere financial account to your master as if he were God. If you are a student, respect your teachers as if they were God.

These are that the practices that constitute service to the Lord; living your life in this manner attracts God's reward. It creates for you, high chances for prosperity. Whether you are government employed or you are employed by a private body or self-employed. The bottom line is that you have services to render. Do it perfectly as well as if it well to Christ; it induces God's blessings.

In another development, let me explain the meaning of Deuteronomy 28:13, this Bible verse states that you shall be the head and not the tail, and above, not beneath. Many people, especially uninstructed Christians, out of recurring misconception and misconstrued perception of this passage have deliberately refused to work. They refuse serving others as a platform for reaching their desired height. This position is not only unscriptural but self destructive and self-limiting.

The Good News Version of the bible puts it thus:

*"The Lord your God will make you the leader among the nation and not the follower; you will always prosper and never fail if you obey faithfully all his commands that I am giving you today."*
**Deut. 28:13**

This passage does not mean that you will wake up one day and become the manager of the bank, the head of state, the king, the principal etc after having a long time wait, doing nothing. Everybody must start small to grow big. What it means is that – you will have leaders, masters, you will serve them, you will be their follower; but if you do it well, you will not continue to be a follower. You will have qualified to have people serving and following you too; in just the same manner and attitude with which you rendered your service. You must serve, but you can't continue to be a server. You must learn to follow, but you don't have be a follower perpetually.

In order words, as you continue to serve diligently, and in obedience to God, it gets to a time when God pours out His blessings on you as reward for your diligence and faithfulness; thereby making u a leader and no longer a follower, a master, no longer an attendant. Nature is hierarchical; you must serve to be served. The quality of people's services to you is the product of your services to your former masters.

A good follower is a good leader, and a good servant is a good master. If you have not served, you can't be served. The truth is that every successful leader is and remains a faithful follower of God's pattern (Hebrews 8:5). Your services must fit into God's specifications; otherwise, He is not obligated to reward you for it.

# CHAPTER NINE
# STRIVE FOR IT

The word STRIVE means to make attempts, to make every effort, and to give your utmost best. It is positive in all respects, and quite different from its negative counterpart, STRIFE, which engenders rivalry.

**"...A lazy man will never have money, but an aggressive man will get rich."**
**Proverbs 11:16, GNB**

The Reversed Standard Version (RSV) of the Bible puts it this way:
**"A gracious woman gets honor, and violent men get riches."**

In a nutshell, there is a place for STRIVING, in order to lay hold of the divine agenda for prosperity. The terms such as aggressiveness and violence in the context of the Bible verse above, does not connote aggression or violence against a fellow man. It simply means having an indomitable will for success and prosperity. It is being ruthless about your duty/job and against any trait, behavior, vice or culture that may be inimical to achieving success and prosperity in life.

You need to be aggressive or violent against poverty spirit or mentality, laziness, fear, distractions, evil thoughts and counsels, indiscipline, indifference and any such things. It refers to gathering wealth by labour, working hard as much as possible, and letting nothing stop your work, as stated in Proverbs 13:11. You must be aggressive and violent enough to overcome oppositions to your blessings. You are to take critical steps of faith and actions, to acquire your desires, even in the face of difficulties. Don't be too gentle! We are in a world of powers, your movement must carry force, (Matt. 11:12).

## WHY STRIVE?
The following are three reasons that call for strive:

A. **The gate is narrow:** the gate to every good thing is usually narrow. Only those who strive can scale through it into abundance.

   *"strive to enter by the narrow door, for many, I tell you, will seek to enter, and will not be able."*

**Luke 13:24, RSV**

This means that you have to be strong in the Lord in order to walk into success. Note that, strive is neither strife nor struggle.

B.  **Building up the church:** men must have to strive, for the church to go forward. There are too many gentle pastors and Christian leaders today. That is why the churches are now in bondage. That is why the witches and wizards are controlling and dictating what happens in the church. That is why an ungodly traditional leader will decree that there should be no vigil prayers and it will stand. Men must be ready to strive if the church must grow. Success without strive is almost a free gift which is unrealistic. Apostle Paul admonishes us, saying, *"...strive to excel in building up the church"* 1 Cor. 14:12, RSV.

C.  **To see God:** it takes serious and sincere strive to see God, as implied by striving for PEACE and HOLINESS with all men; being the fundamental requirements for any man to see God. Do you know what it takes to STRIVE? It is to live a holy life, to forgive and live in peace with all men, and to conquer the flesh for Christ. The author of the book of Hebrews understood this fact, hence he penned, *"Strive for peace with all men and for the holiness, without which no one will see the Lord"* Heb. 12:14 (RSV).

A successful strive is defined by a sustained effort. Dare to strive positively; there is breakthrough by so doing. Strive on, push through, press on, stay on the task, keep fighting, and remember to give one more try, always. That is how to strive! "Press on: obstacles are seldom the same size tomorrow as they are today" (Robert Schuller). Strive makes you have persistent desire to accomplish what you have to do, and to receive your entitlements. Williams F. kumuyi once said "persistent hunger and thirst for the deep things of God can banish luke-warmness." I absolutely concur! Don't forget, **strive stumbles storms into springs of success.** In as much as you are encouraged to strive, it is pertinent to mention that you are not prosperous because you have strived only, but because God has decided to bless you after all, the race is not for the swiftest, nor he that wills, it God Who shows mercy.

# CHAPTER TEN
## SOFT PEDAL FOR IT

The blessing of God is not "a do or die" affair. Ecclesiastes 8:6 says that there is way to get things done, but very little does man know. If God does not help a man, nothing and nobody else can help him. If you are not blessed, you are indeed not and no matter how hard you work, you can't make hands meet. Prosperity is God given and it comes in measures, grades and perspectives. God's prosperity agenda is time-bound. You have to understand your time and take hold of it. There is no cause for alarms, if all your buddies seem to be ahead of you. It is not about who gets what first, it is about God unfolding and delivering your portion you according to Hive divine orchestrations. You must not acquire landed properties this year, you must not get married this year, your must not purchase your own car this year, if God has not designed it so. We must learn to take every step in the WILL and counsel of God. If you have not heard from Him, then ensure that you make no moves. Soft pedal, don't be faster than God in your quest for success and prosperity.

**"Every man also to whom God has given wealth and possessions and power to enjoy them, and to accept his lot and find enjoyment in his toil - this is the gift of God."**

**Eccl. 5:19, RSV**

It is crystal clear that, it is one thing to get wealth and yet another, to enjoy it. Only God can make both happen; to make you prosper and empower you to enjoy the prosperity and fruits of your labour. Thus, it is important to soft pedal. Pause a moment and listen to God. Don't be faster than the moves of God. Never attempt to be ahead of God in His Scheme of Work. You may have plans, but it's God that blesses it (Prov. 16:3). If God doesn't bless your plans, you can't be successful in carrying them out. God must direct your actions if you must succeed (Prov. 16:9). Therefore, soft pedal! Hard work outside God's Scheme of Work is like chasing the wind. God has a program for you. Go and inquire from Him and then follow it, no matter how slow it appears, stick to it.

If you have sincerely strived, without head ways, then it points to either one or more of these three reasons:

a. You are probably striving for the wrong things
b. You are probably striving for the right things at the wrong time, or
c. You are probably striving for the wrong things at the wrong time.

Once you discover which of the above reasons is implicated, one thing becomes indispensable - going back to the drawing board. Return to God, the Author and Finisher of your faith and then soft pedal. God wants to bless you; He desires your ultimate wellness and prosperity. I am very sure of this point. But soft pedal! Only the things that are revealed by God belong to man. It is the gift of the Lord to work hard and enjoy the fruits thereof.

"So I turned about and gave my heart up to despair over all the toil of my labors under the sun, because sometimes a man who has toiled with wisdom and knowledge and skill must leave all to be enjoyed by a man who did not toil for it. This also is vanity and a great evil. What has a man from all the toil and strain with which he toils beneath the sun? For all his days are full of pain, and his work is a vexation; even in the night his mind does not rest. This also is vanity. There is nothing better for a man than that he should eat and drink, and find enjoyment in his toil. This also, I saw, is from the hand of God; **for apart from him who can eat or who can have enjoyment? For to the man who pleases him God gives wisdom and knowledge and joy; but to the sinner he gives the work of gathering and heaping, only to give to one who pleases God.** This also is vanity and a striving after wind."

Eccl. 2:20-26, RSV

Those who pursue success, wealth and prosperity outside God, do so at a detrimental cost. They simply end at gathering and heaping the resources or finished products, while those who work after the law of Christ take their turns in enjoying it. That is, in the actual sense, the evil doers are working for the righteous to enjoy.

# CHAPTER ELEVEN
## SOW FOR IT

To sow is to plant, it also refers to investing, putting in something, laying a foundation, establishing a base or root for something. To sow also means to give. You sow seeds! When we talk about sowing, we must also talk about seeds and harvests. They are observed at different seasons, such that the sowing/planting season necessarily has to precede the harvest season.

A farmer that has not sown does not have a hope of harvest. He reaps a good mango if a man sows a healthy mango seed. After sowing some seeds, the quality of your harvest depends on the quality and viability of the seeds. I think the principle of "sowing" and "reaping" summarizes all matters associated with prosperity. You reap what you sow, Eccl. 12:14. The outcome of today is directly and exactly the product of yesterday's input. What you get is in direct proportionality to what you have given.

Please I want you to understand this point very well: what you call luck today is the reward, or if you like, the harvest of previous seeds sown or works accomplished. There is just not a thing that happens by chance, nobody can build a mansion in the air without a foundation, except in the mind alone. When there is disappointment here and there, and someone else is appointed, he or she should not best be defined as lucky, he is only blessed by God and has most likely sown similar seeds previously. We know that there could be manipulations somewhere, to keep people at a spot all through life; but should it affect Christians?

Today, we have more of best wishers and time wasters than winners. To be a winner, you must first sow winning attitude in your speech, thought, relationship, and the likes. There is no such thing as "overnight success". The success that happens in the night is as a result of the success seed sown in the day, and vice versa. Don't remain a wisher, sow something. And adage says that if wishes were horses, beggars would ride. Most people who simply sat at a spot and wished themselves good things, have never lived to have it. And so it will always be. The future leans on the present, and the present leans on the past. Those that hope for a brighter future cannot emphatically have it if the action of the present does not dictate so. If you want a better future, sow one today.

Many Christians are financially poor today because they claim to have faith, but without actions. Listen, you have got the power to create your most desired future. Even when all the success principles fail, that of "sowing and reaping," "cause and effect" or "action and reaction" remains valid. Isaac Newton defines it well when he said that there was always an opposite but equal reaction to every action. You make a living by what you get; you make a life by what you give.

Brethren, every great venture starts as a dream, but it stops (dies) there without appropriate actions. That is the problem with many believers. The hand must be on the plough. Only those that sow in tears are qualified to reap in joy. Only those that refuse to quit sowing the right seed can find their time of God's blessings. Don't envy successful people and tag them lucky. Ask them not why, but how. Then sow the same seed, and you will get the same result. I assure you!

In Asia, there is a particular tree called the great giant bamboo, this bamboo has very hard seeds, owing to the hardness of the seed, when sown (into the soil) it must have to be fertilized and properly watered each day that passes for four consecutive years. Only this exercise enables it to break the soil (germinate). In the fifth year the tree becomes visible or seen by passers-by. Remarkably, it is capable of growing at rates as fast as four feet in just a day, once it breaks the soil. This is such that in about a month (actually less than a month), its height becomes incredibly about nine feet.

An undiscerning individual would call this "overnight success" or "luck" counting only the days of extra-ordinary growth. Actually, you will agree with me that the bamboo grew to that height in five solid years and not in 30 days, as it now appears.

There is always a story (sowing) before every glory (growing). It is sowing that takes precedence to growing, but unfortunately, only few persons understand this. Majority of people is interested in just the glory and not the story, but the story is always a ladder to the glory. The story you are not willing to listen to is the glory you will never obtain. Learn to pay the PRICE by sowing. The price you pay commensurate the prize you receive. No price, no prize! It is that simple. If successful students, like others in other areas, tell you how much they have to read (the lot they have to go through) to get to where they are now, I know that most people who envy them will instantly change their mindsets.

By and large, every good thing you do in secret mostly, is a sown seed, every mark or display of sincerity, truthfulness, honesty, kindness, divine love is a seed sown to your credit; just keep at it, the truth you speak today (as a seed) can grow and make you reap a ministerial political appointment when you would not even look in that direction and then, people will call it luck. No good deed is a waste – it must produce better, if you keep at it. Go the long haul, pay the full price, sow the full seed, it sets you on the way to rich and plenteous harvest. Your long periods of failure, back-breaking hard – work, countless buckets of sweat and intensive brain racking cannot go unrewarded. You can acquire you desire if you can sow the right seed at the right time, the only right time is NOW!

**"He who observes the wind will not sow; and he who regards the clouds will not reap. In the morning sow your seed, and at evening withhold not your hand; for you do not know which will prosper, this or that, or whether both alike will be good."**

**Eccl. 11:4, 6, RSV**

Seed sowing is a sure way to provoking divine interventions. Keep sow and you will keep reaping. Somebody once said to us in a class, that whatever was not enough to accomplish his project automatically became a seed in his hand. He said it to demonstrate how addicted he had become to seed sowing, and he never lacked a thing, true to God's Word. Apostle Paul said, "I have planted, Apollos watered; but God gave the increase" (1 Corinthians 3:6, KJV).

From the aforementioned scriptural verse, you can see that in the school of abundance and prosperity, until man's role in completely performed, God is not permitted to act. God can only bless the work of your hands. Jesus needed the bread and fish to multiple and provide for the multitude. God need Moses to stretch forth the rod in his hands, to part the red sea. It is our responsibility to give God reasons to bless us. Unless you plant or sow (like Paul), God will have nothing to increase.

Therefore, every man expecting an increase or promotion in any field of life MUST learn to sow seeds.

# CHAPTER TWELVE
# THE "WEPWAP" FORMULA FOR RECEIVING

WePWaP stands for: **We**ed, **P**lant, **Wa**tch and **P**reserve. Here, we are going to consider the principle applied by any successful farmer which is also applicable to life issues generally. The first thing that comes to the mind of a farmer is the type of seed to cultivate when the land is already secured. No matter how large the area of the farm land you have acquired is, without seeds, it lies fallow and unproductive.

The issue is that you must have the SEED to sow. The most unfortunate people are those who think that they have no seed to cultivate, the truth is that, in life, everybody has a SEED to sow. It lies right there in you, as a talent or potential, touch it and tell it that you are going to the field to work with it – to sow it. On the other hand, your life is a viable seed. Your life and what it takes to keep your on physically, are undeniable seeds. What I mean is that, you can actually invest it to get something far better. Just talked about those who will at last find life (i.e. true meaning to life), as those who sow (or temporally lose) their physical life.

Now, when a farmer gets the seed, this formula (WePWaP) comes to play. In the case that this formula is abused, with little or no regards to the viability or potency of the seed and the fertility of the soil, the harvest will be very poor – the desired result will cease to manifest. Therefore, assuming that you have been able to harness the man-power and the available resources needed to become great, assuming that you have succeeded in identifying your seeds and field of specialization and are ready to sow, the following must be strictly adhered to in order to achieve the target of receiving God's blessing and good harvest of prosperity, longevity and all other benefits.

## WEED – Matthew 15:13

This goes beyond, removing unwanted grasses and trees; it includes, preparation of the ground for sowing, willingness to pay the cost price, being decisive and putting in place the necessary tools for effective the required adventure. By weeding, you are exploring the opportunities available and harnessing the resources at hand for judicious utilization.

This is meant to imply that, even when the whole resources are made available but the ground remains unprepared, it hinders the sowing exercise; you can't sow anything on it. By extension, if your mind is not thoroughly prepared, you may get discouraged along the line, and end up not getting to the harvest season.

In this light, to be successful in everything you do, you must learn to prepare. Preparation is crucial to every worthwhile adventure. The farmers have seasons for preparing the land. When this is undone as and due, the farmer business will not augur well. I have not seen any student who wrote an examination without preparing but passed triumphantly. Ben Carson prepared for six months before he operated on the Siamese twins. Weeding gives you the opportunity to create a vision. You can only cultivate the area of land that you have weeded (prepared).

In every facet of life, to grow, weeding is necessary, when you are not prepared, opportunities will come and go without your knowing it. Preparation is the first law of opportunity. Most people that complain today have not prepared adequately; they have not weeded and so, they can't see job opportunities anywhere and everywhere.

Adequate preparation is the background for lasting prosperity. It is a period when you define your strength and when to employ helpers. No good artist goes to the stage to perform without first playing the scripts. That is preparation! You have had too many failures and disappointments because you have not prepared well enough. As a teacher, you have not taught well because you have not prepared well. Whoever you are, you have not made good and successful speech in public because you have not prepared well enough. Sufficient preparation makes success a possibility; though I should be quick to say that success in life does not entirely rest on it. But it is a necessary phenomenon which we must all imbibe to qualify for success.

In another development, weeding which also signifies "clearing," is symbolic of the removal of the unwanted and unnecessary things on the wheel of your success. During weeding, you select your friend and possibly drop some; you identify and avoid the unfriendly friends. Any so called friend that does not contribute to your growth, or reveal to you or challenge your abilities positively, should be dropped. I discovered that 61% of the success or failure of student are traceable to their choice of friends. If you must acquire the blessings of God, then you have to weed out the possible obstacles. They could be human or material. As a student, persons who do not share the same vision as you shouldn't be your best friends. It does not mean that they are bad; it is just that they do not fit into your life. Note that cassava in a yam farm is a weed and unwanted. Be wise!

Everything that is good is not good for you, so also, every brilliant or intelligent person may not be good for you as a friend. In preparing to receive from God, you must also check your character and "weed" were necessary. Those who willingly wish to win must winnow with their wings. You are to prepare the ground for God's blessings. It is your duty to create a niche for yourself in God's divine agenda for long life and prosperity. It is your responsibility to build up your capacities to carry God's blessings. Until you have weeded, you are not permitted to plant.

## PLANT – Jeremiah 1:10

When you have finished clearing (weeding), you go ahead to make your ridges or bed, and ready to plant. To plant means to establish, to invest or to ground. Invariably when you are planting, you are actually giving. If a farmer does not give to the soil (by planting), he/she does not expect any harvest. Christians must learn to give to or invest in other people by faith; financially, academically, morally and otherwise. We too, should be ready to be sold out by God, for the salvation of souls. We must work hard to be truly seeds in God's empyreal Hands.

In any case when you give, you are planting. Now, a farmer does not wait until he/she gets the full amount of seed required to cover the farm before he/she starts planting. In the same way, you must start your investment with whatever seed you have. If you have little money make sure you invest. If you have little knowledge and ability go ahead and plant, don't wait till you have more than enough; because seasons change. The person who needs your service today may not necessarily need it tomorrow; why don't you help out now that you have the opportunity. You can start help by giving small but don't hate to give big. Once again, give; plant as soon as you have the opportunity, the season may change. Every occasion to give is a privilege.

This stage is the most critical stage. It is a decision making point. This phase offers you the right to define and determine you own destiny. Whatever you plant, is what stands. It is an endorsed open check; care must be exercise so as not to make a grievous mistake. It is the fruit of whatever you plant (sow) that you will reap. Good for good, best for best and worst for worst. Nobody has harvested blessings after planting a curse. You must be careful with what you say and do because by your utterances you can sow seed weather good or bad. It will germinate and definitely produce fruits of its own kind. You have been given the power to plant the kind of future or destiny you want for yourself. You cannot feature in the future you cannot picture. The kind of seed you plant is the picture of the kind of future you want for yourself. If you plant the best, there are high chances that you will reap the best, plant well to get well. Nevertheless, unless you are watchful, whatever you plant can be uprooted by an enemy.

**WATCH – Mark 14:38**

To watch in this context is to protect. You have to protect the seed you have sown. You must not sleep or allow someone else to destroy your seeds. Don't allow circumstances or hardships to do it. You must protect or watch over your integrity it attracts God blessings. You have to be careful so that people do not destroy the image you have taken time to build over the years. The easiest way to be dragged into this mud is compromise. Don't compromise!

Another way of watching is to provide nourishment for the seeds you have sown. This can be cheaply achieved through constant praying and studying of the Bible. You should be able to sustain your growth and faith through the knowledge of the Word of God. When you remain nourished and obedient to God, you are preparing yourself to take your solid place in His prosperity agenda. There is an inevitable need to watch, otherwise you will fail and miss His plans for your life. May that not be your portion in Jesus' name!

*"Watch ye, stand fast in the faith, quit you like men, be strong."*
**1 Corinthians 16:13, KJV**

*"Be watchful, stand firm in your faith, be courageous, be strong."*
**1 Corinthians 16:13, RSV**

Watch over your character and your relationship with God. Praise God!

Let me introduce you to one important aspect of watching, which is WAITING. Waiting for harvest is the actual thing after planting. While watching, you are in the real sense waiting for God's time of reward or harvest for your labour. It is the waiting season that comes after sowing. This season is a period of corrections, rebukes, alignments, adjustments and actions. You don't crinkle your arms while waiting and still expect to blossom in business (Proverbs 6:10-11). Isaiah 40:31 makes it abundantly clear that God is the ultimate source of strength, divine blessings and all that pertain to life and godliness. Our reward comes from Him alone and is delivered in His own time, called the DUE SEASON. God gives meat in due seasons. King David Jesse said with deep understanding:

**"My soul, wait thou only upon God; for my expectation is from him."**
**-Psalms 62:5, KJV**

**"These wait all upon thee; that thou mayest give them their meat in due season."**
**-Psalms 104:27, KJV**

God is not a magician, you must wait for your seeds to germinate, grow into maturity, produce flowers and fruits, get ripen before you can harvest them. You can't just get what you want because you have done one good, just wait, that good will definitely count at last. God is diligent enough to remember and reward your labours of love (Hebrews 6:10). Just wait on the Lord.

Moreover, no man can please God without faith (Hebrews 11:6); and the proof of our faith is patience - our confidence in His ability to perform His Word in due time. Men of faith are also men of great patience, men who have learnt and mastered the act of waiting on the Lord, no matter the pressure. God demands that we wait on, after doing His Will to obtain His promise (Hebrews 10:36). When waiting close your eyes to the success of others this enables you to grab what is yours when it eventually arrives. In the waiting season of a man, the success of other people can be a very big detour and distraction.

You need to wait patiently. Mike Murdock said, "Everybody's calling is geographical." This means that, God blessing Joseph in Lagos doesn't mean you can only be blessed in Lagos. You don't need to go abroad to be blessed, just do what is right and wait for your God – watch. God keeps saying to those who care to listen, "Watch for the new thing I am going to do..." (Isaiah 43:19, GNB). Abraham waited for a city which had a foundation and its builder being God (Hebrews 11:10, GNB), and today he is in the bosom of the Lord. You and I can do the same, learning from our father in faith, it doesn't fail.

## HOW TO WATCH

1. Pray always (Matthew 26:41; Mark 14:38; 1 Peter 4:7)
2. Study the Bible as often as possible (2 Timothy 2:15; Joshua 1:8)
3. Be careful in all things: speech, friends, words etc. (2 Timothy 4:5)
4. Endure afflictions (2 Timothy 4:5; 1 Peter 2:30)
5. Preach the gospel of truth (2 Timothy 4:2-5)
6. Make full proof of your ministry (2 Timothy 4:5)
7. Work out your salvation with fear and trembling (Phil. 2:12)
8. Don't complain, do your work and just wait (Phil. 2:14)
9. Don't sleep but be sober (Matt. 13:25; 1 Peter 5:8)

Avoid evil desires let alone being drawn and trapped by it (James 1:14-15). Evil desire is the primary route of temptation, man is the manufacturer of temptation because he is usually tempted based on his desires and the state of his mind.

Moreover, the fundamental need to watch is built upon its necessary assistance in overcoming temptation. To stand steady in your faith you need to be watchful. It is through watching that you tend your potentials properly. The period of watching (or waiting) is also the period of divine visitation.

On a final note, the bountiful nature of the harvest (i.e. final outcome) expected has great and direct influence on the decoration of the watching process. Consider for instance, the economic importance of palm tree and that of maize. Also, consider the time lapse before harvest and the weight of the reward from each of them. Great delays produce great delivering. Great obstacles bring forth great miracles. Keep watch! Be focused! God is processing our breakthrough package. He is at work in your favour. The numbers of your years spent watching or waiting is not the ultimate, it is the blessings that it yields that counts. Be encouraged in the Lord. The watching season is the last season before the harvest season. Your harvest time is near; just keep watch!

**PRESERVE- Genesis 19:34, NKJV**

After the colossal harvest, don't be carried away. There is need to preserve some of the seeds of your blessings for the following season. The essential point here is PLAN. You must plan for the next season-to give back to the soil-to sow. If don't invest for the future you may come to find if very rough. When you are blessed today, preserve part of your wealth for the next season (generation) as a seed. This seed is what God will bless. This is the only way your blessings can be sustained.

In another sense, it means to share your wealth with others. GIVE. This in future (as a seed) will grow into blessings for the expansion of the sustenance of your wealth. Set such a foundation for your children and beyond. It will be a very sad story, if you are greatly blessed, but after your death your children begin to harvest curses. Preserve your blessings for your children. It is not a sin. The best way to do this is not to stock up money in the bank and underneath the earth, but it is simply to be good to other people. Be a blessing to other people. That is the whole essence. It also goes to prove that you love God, the giver of wealth.

*"If a rich person sees his brother in need, yet closes his heart against his brother, how can he claim that he loves God?"*
**John 3:17, GNB**

The New International Version (NIV) uses material possessions, but I want to include spiritual possessions also. The riches as used here, is all encompassing. Everybody has his/her area of great riches. Use it well. It pays! If you are not rich financially, then you could be rich in good counsel, words of knowledge, wisdom and understanding; you could be rich in spiritual endowments or gifts, material supplies, words of encouragement or motivation, moral values, divine virtues, academic prowess, peace and joy etcetera. There is no end to riches, everybody is rich. There is no restriction to riches; everybody can be rich in any desired area of life. I am rich! Just look inward, you will discover that you are also. But don't forget; there is a call by God to bless others around us also by our riches. We are blessed to be a blessing to others (Genesis 12:2).

Sincerely, it is a curse, if you are financially rich and people around you are hungry. You yet live in bondage if you are wealthy, but your parents at home wear tattered clothes and can't eat proper three square meals daily. That kind of prosperity has been corrupted. God blesses and adds no sorrow think. When your gift or wealth causes people sorrow or give them cause to regret, then you need serious spiritual examination and deliverance. If your riches do not diffuse to bless other people, then you are in bondage. Remember, your blessing is yet incomplete until you become a blessing to your world (Genesis 12:2-3). You have been blessed to bless others, favoured to favour, helped to help, and lifted to up-lift; anything less than or short of this, is an abuse of God's blessings.

# CHAPTER THIRTEEN
## WHY PEOPLE DON'T RECEIVE, Part One

Many people work hard, others pray hard, some are very diligent and trust sincerely in God; yet they don't receive their heart desires. What could bring a man to this state of life? What keeps a man in the state of perpetual struggles? Having sown precious and viable seeds on a fertile soil, carefully watched over the plants, providing it enough and needed nourishment, what could possibly make the husbandman still meet with very poor harvest? These are the things the Lord will be teaching us in this chapter and the next.

It is not a surprise that a dedicated and devoted pastor, who is an instrument in the Hands of God in blessing the congregation spiritually and otherwise, is as poor as the church rat. Pastor K. C. Warden, very wretched and undignified has been in this situation for many years. He lived by the consolation of common clichés like, "there is time for everything" and "God's time is the best" for 17 years plus 7 months. But God is lovely and merciful; and will always initiate steps to show us our faults and ways of getting out of the messes we find ourselves.

In the 5th month of the 18th year, Pastor Warden's wife and children became obviously fed up and called the attention of their husband and father to their pitiable and contemptible situation. He rebuked them and charged them to have faith. But in the 6th month of that same year, Mrs. Warden grew rebellious, hating their state of abject poverty and threatened to leave him alone in the city for her village with their children, should he would not proffer solution to the ugly state of their lives, as the shepherd of the home.

After that confrontation put up by his wife, Pastor Warden was touched and went into prayers concerning his life. Since then, the following words kept punching his spirit "...you are in the wrong place..." He got perturbed by this persistent ministration and then opened up the next time his wife confronted him. He confessed that he had always rejected his transfer to the village churches nearby, but influencing it to suite his lust. He was fond of manipulating the whole arrangement of the authority of the ministry. So, they prayed together that moment and his wife admonished him to accept any place he was transferred to in the future. The stable prayer point of the family became "Lord, let Your Will be done!"

However, the situation lingered on until the 21st day of the 7th month, when he got a letter of transfer again, to a more interior village. Without choice, they accepted gladly, and in a matter of days they left the city for the village, they moved their last set of luggage on the 31st of July that year. In a matter of three months later, their situations changed, their story changed. All the positive changes they experienced were traceable to: (1) Their obedience to God, living in the centre of His Will (2) the location of their place of allocation. They were where they were sent, the right place. May the LORD open your eyes as He instructs us on the reasons why people don't receive in Jesus' name.

Don't be surprise because your own case may be similar. There are very many reasons why people don't receive from God, let's look at some of them under the following sub-topics.

**CLOSED HEAVENS**

When the heavens are closed over a man, no matter how much he tries, nothing works for him. The soil becomes hard, helpers treat him with contempt, his paths become thorny and over grown with grass, his vision becomes blurred (if he does not become totally blind), he labours much but reaps very little, he toils like the elephant but eats like the ant, he works and makes investment but for other people to enjoy, whatever he does, fails, he is constantly greeted with disappointments and delays, frustration visits him very often, he becomes best of friend with poverty and lack. That is a man under a closed heaven. It is a miserable experience.

The shutting of the heavens ceases the availability of rain and water (2 Chronicles 7:13). The already existing brooks or source of nourishment gets dried up (1 Kings 17:7). The fruitfulness of our efforts, livestock and vineyard is adversely affected when the heavens are closed (Haggai 1:11). The subjects of the sources, the evidences, the causes and the effects of a closed heaven have been graciously discussed in the book, "Securing Open Heavens," by Godday O. Aghedo.

**DWELLING IN THE WRONG PLACE**

No matter how much you try in the wrong place, you cannot prosper, everybody has a ministry which is meant to make us work and obtain God's blessing. It becomes a herculean task to reach this level of God's blessings, if you are in the wrong ministry or field. This is also applicable to students who have the tendency of choosing and studying the wrong degree courses. They can't get fulfillment like that. Dwelling in the wrong place offers you the wrong expectations. Don't be enticed, and don't be deceived by other people's callings; face your ministry, for that is where you can find your blessings.

"Everybody's calling is geographical," says Mike Murdock. This is true because though God can bless any man anywhere, the wrong place will influence you wrongly into getting a wrong result, something akin to the story of Pastor Warden above. Every time spent in the wrong place amounts to a total waste. Understand your ordained place of assignment and the content of your responsibility.

Noah was saved because he entered the ark – the right place. Abraham was blessed because he was always in the right place, following the voice of God. The prodigal son became poor because he went to spend his money in the wrong place. Many people have died in the wrong places, many have suffered in the wrong profession and many still are struggling. God's grace cannot accompany a man to where God has not sent him.

Jacob understood this fact, hence he said to his family: "we are going to leave here and go to bethel…" Genesis 35:3. In verse 6, they arrived at Bethel and in verses 10-15, he was blessed by God.

Please, you must leave where you are now for your Bethel. That is where God will bless you. Bethel is a place of revelation, divine visitation, rescue and the land of promise, the Canaan land. If you don't leave here, you can't live there. The difference between THERE and HERE is "T" which stands for TRAVEL. Thus, you must travel to get there. Make a move, take a step!

You can't be blessed for working where God has not called you to be. If I send you to work in my cassava farm, and you end up working in my neighbours' farm; I have to obligation to pay you as well as my neighbour. Ask yourself: am I in the wrong place? If YES, don't hesitate, leave immediately to your Bethel.

## SIN

Sin is disobedience to the Lord. Proverbs 28:9 says that the prayer of a sinner is an abomination to the Lord. In verse 13 it says,

*"He who covers his sins will not prosper, but whoever confesses and forsake them will have mercy"* (KJV).

*"You will never succeed in life if you try to hide your sins...."*
**Proverbs 28:13, GNB**

Avoid sin, be no more a slave to it. Many people still live in secret sin; I don't need to tell them why they've not prospered in their disciplines. Secret sins make your blessings to remain in the secret. It is a destroyer also, confess it, forsake it, you will have mercy and you will meet your breakthrough. SIN is an acronym for Self Imposed Nature. You have power over sin since when Jesus Christ won the victory for us on the cross. Sin shouldn't be your master, it is dangerous. It has nothing to offer other than death (Romans 6:23). Indeed, SIN is a reproach to any person. No spirituality immunes anybody against this effect of sin. It is a serious barrier to the blessings of God (Proverbs 14:34). "The guilt of sin is not removed, if the gain of sin is not restored" (Matthew Henry).

## WRONG MOTIVES

*"When you ask, you do not receive, because you ask with the wrong motives, that you may spend what you get on pleasures"*
**James 4:3, NIV**

This is the problem of many people. It is unambiguously clear that if you want God's blessings simply because of the pleasure of it, that is, personal pleasure, you can't have it. I see the blessings of God as a possibility for anybody to obtain, but it has to be seen as a privilege to have it at one's disposal and then as being in charge of its equitable distribution. When God blesses a man, the ideal thing is that He has answered the prayers of many millions of people around that man.

Nobody can deceive God, He is not fooled, and it is the Lord that judges your motives (Proverbs 21:2). He knows and He weighs the intent of the heart of man. If the intent is to oppress others, you can't receive; if it is to intimidate others or initiate strife you can't receive; if it is to show off, forget receiving anything from God; your motives must be right. Proverbs 21:27 says that God hates receiving sacrifices from wicked men, especially when they do it with evil (wrong) motives; then how much more impossible it is for a wicked man to receive with wrong motives.

We are freely in this world, not in competition with anybody but ourselves individually. Therefore, if your request is built on being able to strike a balance with the standards of ungodly men, then don't expect to receive. You are not in a competition with any man except the YOU in you, not even the YOU of yesterday. If you can streamline your motives, for good, you can stimulate receiving treasures from God. The right motives should be to bless the work of God, to bless other people in our world or sphere of contact. It is not a true success, if your success does not give people joy. If the people round you cannot sincerely mention that you are rich (by your generosity); then you are sincerely poor, not rich. You are blessed to bless, uplifted to uplift, you are saved to save and you are enriched to make others rich. Anything short of this kind of motive is wrong and it hinders God's blessings.

## DEAFENED TO THE CRY OF THE POOR

When a man refuses to listen to the cry of the poor, God will not also listen to him.
*"If you refuse to listen to the cry of the poor, you own cry for help will not be heard."*
**Proverbs 21:13, GNB**

Do not ever despise the poor. Help them as much as your ability can carry; this way, God can hear your own cry. This is my philosophy: the rich need more helps from God than the poor; so have respect for the poor, pay attention to them and be loyal to friends. Let's close with the words of the greatest philosopher, "The rich and the poor have this in common: the Lord made them both" Proverbs 22:3, GNB. The twenty-eighth chapter verse twenty seven of proverbs says that many people will curse you if you close your eyes to the poor; but never in need is he that gives to the poor or pays attention to them. Here is a true talk: Spiritual forces rise up against you anytime you refuse to see the poor around you. They are at times, the so called princes of Persia that will hinder you from receiving from God, don't wait until they present themselves before you nor until their cries become so loud that it can cause temporary deafness. "The Lord has given us eyes to see with and ears to listen with" Proverbs 20:12, GNB.

## SELF CENTEREDNESS

Self-centeredness is a hindrance to obtaining from God as well as a killer of already acquired blessings. Self-centered people are those that operate by the principle of "I", "ME", "MY" and "MINE" only. They find it extremely difficult to get anything from God. When you are egocentric, you become blind to the prosperity opportunities God sends your ways; as a result, you remain where you are. God's blessings and prosperity packages must not be seen as a private property. Self-centeredness is the shortest and easiest way to let poverty into your house. When you obstruct the flow of the blessings of God at you end, you are invariably withholding; this only leaves you poorer (Proverbs 11:24, KJV).

Paul admonished the people of Philippi to do nothing with selfish ambitions or vain conceits or cheap desires to boast (Philippians 2:3). The only valid proof that you have to show that you are not self-centered is to esteem others better than yourself; this is simply humility, not inferiority complex or very low self-esteem. It is neither self-depression nor self-relegation; it only shows that you have the mind of Christ and that you share in His nature (Philippians 2:5-9).

Let me ask you: Are you egocentric? Are you selfish and narrow minded? Well don't jump at any conclusion yet; you can judge that correctly from the placements or order of priority you have given to God, other people and yourself, in your private life. The true order should be – God first, others second and self, third. Any alteration in this arrangement show that you are selfish or self-centered to a dangerous degree. Jesus did not try to become equal with God, though He would be right to take such positions (Philippians 2:6-7). We must learn to be people oriented in our quest to feature in God's long life and prosperity agenda.

## MARKS OF SELF – CENTEREDNESS – Philippians 2

a. Driven by selfish ambition (vs. 3)

b. Promotion of vain glory (vs. 3)

c. Boastful desires and tendencies (vs. 3; Proverbs 27:1-2)

d. Self-projection, self-announcement and self-aggrandizement (vs. 3)

e. Practice of favouritism, nepotism and discriminatory inclinations. These folks claim to be extremely adherent to Galatians 6:10. It is dangerous to be at the extremes, you know it. By practice, these persons prefer to give jobs to unqualified relations, rather than a qualified stranger. That is unjust! They rob Peter to pay Paul. At any cost, even to the detriment of other folks outside their family, they ensure that they favour their own. They hold the opinion that, any good deed done to an outsider is a loss. This is the attitude of gross selfishness.

f. Always in a hurry to get rich, but gets poverty instead (Proverbs 28:22)

g. Working is isolation, doing things alone, wanting to succeed alone, very high conservativeness, and excessive respect for privacy. Self-centered people don't believe in partnership. Everything is personal to them; they hate to share glories, laurels, commendations, successes, positions and gifts with other people.

h. They are callous naturally – hating to see others progress. When others get things done, they wonder why it was not them. They go ahead to discredit the other persons, cooking up reasons why the other persons couldn't have achieved that feat, were it not luck.

No doubt these attributes above, have physical and spiritual powers to deter anybody from partaking in God's prosperity agenda.

# CHAPTER FOURTEEN
## WHY PEOPLE DON'T RECEIVE, Part Two

The Bible records that all things that pertain to life and godliness have been have given to us, according to His divine power, through the knowledge of Him that has called us to a life of glory and virtue (2 Peter 1:3). God has called us to His glory and excellence, and has made available everything that I will ever need to live a life of godliness. But these provisions are readily accessed through KNOWLEDGE. That means that IGNORANCE is also a reason why people do not receive from the Lord. Knowledge is a key to the treasure house of God. There is a life God wants us to live – a long life, a prosperous life, a healthy life, a glorious life, a virtuous life, an excellent life, a life full of success records, an impactful life and above all, a godly life.

Note that, a sickly life is not godly, a poverty smitten life is not godly, premature death is not godly, consistent failure is not godly, stagnation is not godly, mysterious loss of valuables and treasures is not godly, and a wanting and lacking life is not godly. It is not enough to be prosperous in the spirit and the salvation of our souls, we should also prosper materially and physically; this is the will of God for us.

*"Beloved, I pray that you may prosper in all things and be in health, just as your soul prospers."*

**3 John 2, NKJV**

Friend, we must stay strong in the Lord and be determined to see His will come to pass in our lives. I refuse to allow anything outside God's Word to reign in my life. Everything He says in His Word is true, I believe it and I am entitled to walk in its reality. Long life is real, divine health is real and kingdom prosperity is real and I will walk these realities. Alleluia!

In chapter thirteen above, we examined six of the factors that often hinder people from receiving their heart desires from God; to include: Closed Heaven, Dwelling in the Wrong Place, Sin, Wrong Motives, Paying Deaf Ears to the Cry the Poor and Self-Centeredness. In this last chapter, we shall consider a few more factors that are very inimical to receiving from God.

## LAZINESS

Laziness is a spiritual disease which can be cured only by hard work. A dose of discipline and hard work drives laziness far beyond reach. God can't work with a lazy or slothful man. They can't receive from Him because God knows that they can't manage whatever He gives to them. They are insensitive and have lost their perceptive power. They have great desires but get nothing.

*"No matter how much a lazy person may want something, he will never get it…"*
**Proverbs 13:4, GNB**

This is because the lazy man has no seed which God will bless. God is not partial, lazy people should learn a lesson from the life of the ants (Proverbs 6:6). God hides His face from a lazy man. He may seek hard, but never finds. God does not listen to lazy people because they don't even have the strength to cry out aloud enough to His hearing. Avoid laziness; it is ungodly because God our Father does not have it in Himself.

This is the basis of laziness – losing all zealous yearning. LAZY is actually an acronym for Lost All Zealous Yearnings. When you have lost all zealous yearnings for hard work, fellowship with brethren, studying the Word of God, prayers at mid night, evangelism, good works, visitation to brethren; then you are lazy. At this point, your cries for help, prosperity, and success may not be loud enough to reach God, you may not be heard. Laziness is the first infirmity that strikes before backsliding invades, and many people leave the church not because the truth is not preached but because they are LAZY. They find the truth too hard to chew.

Parents and guardians must teach their children and wards respectively the consequences of laziness. The culture of discipline has to be resurrected and taught practically and sincerely, the place of hard work in God's prosperity agenda must be truthfully spelt out. The detrimental effects of getting labourers to do all the works you have to do both at home and at the farm or business arena, far outweigh its seeming benefits on your children or wards. Let them get to work out things too, they should be given the opportunity to learn, they should be allowed to get their hands in the mud and work. Any achievement or success that is not standing on tough times cannot withstand tough times. The crux of the matter is that, a lazy man can't receive from God!

Laziness is a letter of invitation sent by a lazy man to poverty, which poverty gladly honours as promptly as possible. Some six remarkable qualities of lazy people are:
> a. They like to sleep and hate work (Proverbs 6:10)
> b. They love to be at ease, they are lovers of pleasures (i.e. all day/time rest; Proverbs 6:10)
> c. They prefer already cracked kernels which are not easy to come by, to cracking some of the numerous un-cracked kernels. That is, they are too lazy to put food in their own mouth. They have the "microwave" mentality (Proverbs 26:15)
> d. They are destroyers and wasters of resources (Proverbs 18:9)
> e. They always procrastinate, they live by wishes instead of by faith (Eccl. 11:4-6; Proverbs 20:4)
> f. They always think and believe that they are wiser than all. They are the wisest in their own eyes (Proverbs 26:12, 16).

Cross-check yourself! Examine yourself thoroughly.

## CONSEQUENCES OF LAZINESS

> 1. It makes you stagnant and dormant like a door swinging on its hinges - Proverbs 26:14
> 2. It makes you an all-time-slave (a perpetual servant) – Proverbs 12:24
> 3. It makes you very poor – Proverbs 10:4
> 4. It constantly pushes you into difficulties and troubles. A lazy man has more thorns to contend with in life – Proverbs 15:19
> 5. It leaves you cripple and helpless – a sort of incapacitation. A lazy man is friendless because he has nothing to offer - Proverbs 19:6

Dear reader, shun laziness and remain unfriendly to whoever encourages it. It corrupts character. Majority of the gentlemen on the road are into such heinous and unsocial acts because they are lazy; not because there are no jobs. Hard work teaches a man to be patient even when there are temporary no jobs.

## UNBELIEF

Unbelief is simply lack of faith or to be without faith. No one can even please God without faith (Hebrews 11:6). In Mark 9:23 Jesus Christ clearly states that everything is possible for him who believes. Unbelief is the creator of impossibilities in people's lives.

When little trials strike, we tend to forget the greatness and abilities of God; thereby panicking. What God wants is that we simply believe in the One (His Son - Jesus) He has sent (John 6:29). Unbelief stages, when we have lost all confidence in Jesus Christ. This is rather than weakness described as unfortunate. Just as a farmer believes that when he/she plants his/her corn in a few days it will germinate and a sick person believes that when he/she takes his/her drugs, he/she will get well, Christians can get everything they want by just believing (faith) in Jesus. Unbelief is one of the most destructive afflictions of a spiritual man. Unbelief is a friend of DOUBT. Doubt is derived from the devil to diligently deceive, deprive and deny Christians God's blessings. Doubters are double minded and can't receive ANYTHING from God (James 1:6-8).

When you do not believe where God is taking you to, unbelief will take you to somewhere else (which you will not like). Belief gives you a sense of focus and specificity of purpose. If you cannot decide and define how you will end, the devil will do it for you, to end anyhow. If you cannot determine where you are going to, you will detach somewhere premature. Build up your faith IN GOD; it is like a ticket to withdraw from His unquantifiable treasure of goodness.

## HOW TO OVERCOME UNBELIEF

1. Study the scriptures regularly – Romans 10:17. Faith comes from hearing the Word of God. Listen to messages (anointed tapes), listen to testimonies, watch miracles, be at live miracle/healing events of God's anointed servants and read Christian literatures by anointed ministers.

2. Don't neglect the gathering of believers – Hebrews 10:25. Attend fellowship always. This a good place to hear God's Words and people's testimonies that will grow your faith.

3. Regularly read about the mighty deed of God both in the old and new testaments. Recount His blessings His miracles and recorded extraordinary performances. Praise His greatness, imagine His power of creation, and imagine how He laid the foundation of the earth. Think of those horrible conditions you have survived in the past. Then believe that He cannot disappoint you now, if He didn't then. Just continue to find reasons to praise Him, even if not directly about you; but at least you heard or read about it of other people. Refresh your memory of the testimonies you have heard or read about, and worship Him.

4. Go back to the scriptures, read the promises of God concerning your situation. Repeat it! Repeat it aloud! Prophesy it upon yourself! Claim it by fixing your name where necessary. And possibly, if you are alone, believing that God is talking to you particularly, shout it out continuously until you have peace in your mind.

5. Pray ceaselessly. Unbelief dies, on the altar of constant prayer, because in the place of prayer we are changed into the very personality of God. We are assured of His presence and are emboldened to function in our full capacities as kings and queens who reign. Constantly pray the prayer of the apostles:

"....make our faith great" Luke 17:5 (GNB)

"....increase our faith" Luke 17:5 (NIV)

Personalize it. Only God can help the unbelief of a man. Living sincerely by these rules on daily basis will indeed conquer your unbelief.

## FORGETTING GOD

Forgetting God does not only hinder us from partaking in His prosperity agenda, it also destroys the blessings already secured. The truth is that when you have the tendency to forget your God because of His blessings, and He discovers it (of course He will), He will not release His treasures on you. It proves you are not yet mature to control divine resources properly and profitably.

Success is also dangerous because it has the power to make people forget God; the One Who had blessed them in the first place. When God discovers this possibility of forgetting Him in you, He delays your portion in the prosperity agenda and then goes on to build you up spiritually, so that you can handle the blessings without being swollen headed.

Premature success kills prematurely. That is why Moses warned the Israelites, not to forget God after He had blessed them.

*"Be careful that you do not forget the lord your God, failing to observe his commands... Otherwise when you eat and are satisfied..., then your heart will become proud and you will forget the Lord your God..."*

**Deut. 8:11-14, NIV**

Every man who goes proud due to God's blessings will consequently be humbled. To overcome pride and the tendency of forgetting God, learn to dwell in the remembrance of the fact that it is God who gives the power to become prosperous (Deut. 8:18). Destruction comes after you forget God (Deut 8:19-20). There is no material thing that lasts, it is God that can sustain it and if we must help Him to sustain it, then it is noteworthy that sustenance of a blessing is only by the same way it was acquired. This means that, if you got your blessings through prayers, you sustain it majorly too, by prayers. The day you stop praying is the day the destruction of the blessing starts. If you got your own believing in God, then, if you stop believing God you have started terminating the life of the blessing.

The trouble is that people forget easily how they started by the time they become great. Never forget you roots. A tree that forgets its root(s) will surely fall. When you get your job by praying and believing in God (i.e. calling on God), but decide to give bribe to get promotion, then, you have forgotten your root (God). You may have the promotion but surely there will be problems. This is why people constantly fall sick; others lose their children, lack of peace in the home, threats by armed-robbers, accidents here and there and the host of such other happenings; which are capable of truncating the essence of the so called promotion.

If there is any evil that does not have direct effect on ones growth in life, it can't be the sin of PRIDE (or forgetting God). Before any sudden fall, goes the slightest seed of pride. Proverbs 16:18 declares that pride is the fundamental cause of every fall and dethronement. As a matter of fact, God resists the proud (1 Peter 5:5), and He humbles (demotes) the proud (James 4:10). Sticking to God consistently induces consistent growth. When you start making results in life, the best way to sustain it is to become more humble before God. Humility at the foot of God is like a well fertilized soil for effective rapid growth. True promotion comes from God. Collin Powell admonished; "don't let your ego get close to your position, so that if you are shot down, your ego doesn't go with it." It simple means that every proud man will be shot down.

Just look around you critically; you will discover somebody who used to do very well but not anymore. Go closer to him/her; try to find out what actually happened. You will discover that the person, if a Christian has deviated from his/her initial commitment to God.

There are several Biblical examples. One familiar example is the life of the great king of Babylon. King Nebuchadnezzar was indeed a powerful king; he was famous and dreaded by the neighbouring communities. He conquered several cities including the city of Jerusalem. God actually gave him the chance to do that; but following his success, at a point he became proud and said:

*"Look how great Babylon is! I built it as my capital city to display my power and right, my glory and majesty."*

**Daniel 4:30, GNB**

He utterly forgot that it was God who let him conquer Jerusalem (Ch. 4:2). This was the foundation of his fall from the throne. What actually happened? He was driven from the throne. He became one of the wild animals (Ox) and lived on grasses in the bush for seven years (Vs. 32-33). A king, what a disgrace! The worst thing that has ever happened to a successful man, I am sure you don't want to fall like Nebuchadnezzar. If true, then, don't forget God; don't give a chance to the smallest seed of pride. It was pride that debased King Nebuchadnezzar.

**"But when his heart was lifted up and his mind hardened in pride, he was deposed from his kingly throne, and they took his glory from him."**

**Daniel 5:20, KJV**

Every enthroned man must kill pride or pride will kill him. God is merciful but when you fall, the best and only thing to do is to run back to God. If you can return to God, you will regain your success, Health and wealth. You can come back to the throne if you can acknowledge God – the giver of your possessions and positions (Daniel 4:26b). Of course, Nebuchadnezzar regained his sanity but not before looking up.

*"When the seven years had passed said the king 'I looked up at the sky, and my sanity returned, I praised the Supreme God and gave honor and glory to the One Who lives forever... No one can oppose His will or question what He does... everything He does is right and just, and He can humble anyone who acts PROUDLY."* (Emphases are mine)

**Daniel 4:34-37, GNB**

Note that, he acknowledged God by looking up to the sky and he got back his sanity; he praised and worshipped God and his throne was given back to him; and he pledge his loyalty and allegiance to God forever. You don't need to be a victim of demotion before you learn. It is better and safer to learn from people's mistakes than from personal ones. Don't forget that, God can humble anyone who acts proudly (Daniel 4:37).

Another example to consider is King Asa. I want you to read the full version of his story from Second Chronicles chapters 14, 15 and 16. When king Abijah died, his son Asa succeeded him as king. Asa started well with God, he pleased the Lord, his God, by doing what was right and good (Ch. 14:2). In 2 Chronicles 14:3; 15:8, 16-18; you see Asa carrying out reform programs, destroying altars of idols, to the point that he removed his grandmother, Maacha from her position as queen. Finally, he went to the extent of entering into a covenant with God.

*"They made a covenant with God, agreed to worship the lord, the God of their ancestors, with all their heart and soul."*

**2 Chronicles 15:12, GNB**

Moreover, they took delight in worshipping the lord, and God gave them peace on every side (Ch. 15:15); this was after they had won very many wars, having God on their side. When the Sudanese attacked with one million men and three hundred chariots, Asa prayed to God for help and they defeated the Sudanese's large army (Ch. 14:9-13). For as long as he anchored his trust on God, he (Asa) had no more wars for the first 35 years of his reign (Ch. 15:19). Does that beat your imagination? The truth is that, if you can trust God enough, you will always have victories over the challenges posed on you by your business, family, academics or marriage etcetera. If there are at all, God himself will take them up. By the Spirit of the Lord, Azariah the son of Oded said to Asa:

*"...The lord is with you as long as you are with him. If you look for him, he will let you find him, but if you turn away, he will abandon you."*

**2 Chronicles 15:1-2, GNB**

May the Lord not abandon you! But, you appear rejected and abandoned whenever you turn away from God and good fate. Asa forget God, that is, Israel forgot God. The protection, power, providence and the defense of the army of God were disregarded. Asa forgot that God has been the source of their immerse victory and peace. He rebelled against God. Instead of God, he relied on the King of Syria. Through in fear, he became proud.

Pride is a terrible thing! Pride is intoxicating. It makes one act foolishly, like a drunkard. A proud man does not walk with his legs but his head. Until it gets done on him, he doesn't take good counsel, he goes on to do more evils to cover for the past evils. He digs his grave himself, he is like a man who is deaf but can only hear himself. Out of an unfeigned love and mercy, the Lord sent Prophet Hanani to King Asa. Yet he didn't retreat, he rather became angry with Hanani and imprisoned him; together with the unleashing of cruelty on the people (2 Chronicles 16:10). The bottom line of the story of King Asa is that, when he forgot God he started having WARS after WARS.

*"The lord keeps close watch over the whole world, to give strength to those whose hearts are loyal to him. You have acted foolishly and so from now on you will always be at war."*

**2 Chronicles 16:9, GNB**

Success is dangerous, when there is the tendency to forget God. Now, consider this sequence of events in the life of Asa:

Asa depended on God and there was no war for the first 35 years of his reign (Ch. 15:19). He forgot God and depended on man (King of Syria) and he became prone to war, because of this, he became crippled by a severe foot disease by the 39th year of his reign. Still unrepentant, he sort helps from doctors rather than God, eventually, two years later (the 41st year of his reign), he gave up the ghost (2 Chronicles 16:11-14).

Beware! This is exactly how those who forget God end their life - in shame. You may not be as lucky as Nebuchadnezzar, who had the chance to repent. Therefore, be sure that you don't forget God when His blessings start manifesting physically in all your endeavours.

God is not partial! The fulfillment of His promises is for all and sundry. Go and get enlisted. There is a list, you must write your name yourself; with a particular pen. The name of the pen is HOLINESS and the name of the paper is PURITY OF THE HEART, the envelope is PATIENCE. Get this pen and paper, write your name neatly on it, envelope it and you will become automatically certified and qualified to receive your package, from above not abroad. Go ahead and take your place in God's long life and prosperity agenda. It is your right and God takes delights in it.

*"...Let the LORD be magnified, Who has pleasure in the prosperity of His servant."*

**Psalms 35:27, NKJV**

Wow! It is pleasurable to God to see you prosper. God is not just interested in your liberty from sin only; He wants to see you live a gleaming life of unending success and prosperity. These are the packages enshrined in our salvation gift, for our decoration and enjoyment. Psalms 149:4, NKJV declares, "For the LORD takes pleasure in His people; He will beautify the humble with salvation." Indeed, salvation is actually for our beautification. In fact, Psalms 132:16 refers to it as clothing. Do not live below standard. Wake up and take your place in the divine agenda for long life and prosperity.

God's Word is infallible! God's covenant of prosperity is forever valid and unfailing. It delivers promptly once the terms and conditions are fully met. One of which is becoming a child of God and Abraham's seed. Once you have fulfilled your part in the covenant of prosperity as a seed of Abraham, God's commitment to it becomes activated. God is ever faithful, even when you are unfaithful. If you fail, God cannot fail. Whether or not His Word is made good in your life, God remains God and trustworthy. The problem is not with God but man. God wants you to live a long life, He wants you to prosper, but it is up to you. You can chose to either be a beggar or a giver, alive or dead, poor or prosperous, sick or healthy, fruitful or barren. I have chosen long life and prosperity.

I am a giver not a beggar…
I have chosen to live out my years fully…
I cannot be sick in my body…
I am a fruitful branch, firmly attached to the vine…
I live in abundance…
I don't lack anything…
No good thing shall be withheld from me…
I am more than a conqueror…
I am the favourite of God…
I have a goodly heritage…
The lines are falling in pleasant places for me…
I am a wonder to my generation…
I am a child of destiny…
I am created for signs and wonders…
I give to nations…
I am above only and never below…
I succeed in the morning, afternoon and the night…
I am the light of the world…
I have good purpose to fulfill on earth…
Without me, the world will be in trouble, so I will live…
Nothing dies in my hands…
Nothing goes down in my hands…
I am blessed of the Lord…
I am a world champion…
The oil and anointing of the Lord is upon me…
I am divinely loaded and packaged to deliver maximally on earth…
I am relevant to my generation and the world at large…
I am needed because I have what the world needs…

I give taste and life to my society...
I am the salt of the earth...
I am the light of the world...

Praise God... If you act on God's Word, He will confirm it. Therefore, succeed, if you want to; and prosper, if you want to. It is absolutely up you. Shalom!

# ABOUT THE AUTHOR

Godday O. Aghedo is an admirable young-star and a Medical Personnel. He is indeed a man of many parts: a distinguished author, counsellor, song composer, poet, leadership expert and highly sought-for inspirational/public speaker.

He is also the author of "Secrets of God's Blessings", and "Securing Open Heavens," many yet to be published manuscripts and more than a few published articles. His leadership acumen has earned him several positions of authority both in secular and sacred institutions alike.

G. O. Aghedo is the founder and president of **Global Multiple Impact Consults (GLOMIC),** which is committed to youth capacity development as well as helping people achieve fulfilment in life.

Made in United States
Orlando, FL
01 February 2024

43165747R00043